THE GENTLE WAY

A SELF-HELP GUIDE FOR THOSE WHO BELIEVE IN ANGELS

TOM T. MOORE

THE GENTLE WAY

A SELF-HELP GUIDE FOR THOSE WHO BELIEVE IN ANGELS

TOM T. MOORE

 Light Technology Publishing

Cover Artist:
Walter Bruneel
www.iasos.com

ISBN 1-891824-60-0

Published by:

800-450-0985
www.lighttechnology.com

Printed by:

PO Box 3540
Flagstaff, AZ 86003

DEDICATION

This book is dedicated to Robert Shapiro. With his wisdom, encouragement and private mentoring—and as I read his published works—I was inspired to create my path by applying to my own life his concepts and practices of benevolent ways, benevolent outcomes, living prayer and love-heat meditation. Robert delivered these books* by speaking with inspiration. He also encouraged my desire to write this book, and I shall be forever indebted to him for helping me to expand upon these concepts, enabling me to bring them to a wider readership and audience. They changed my life and hopefully will change yours as you too begin taking the Gentle Way.

—Tom T. Moore, May 2006

---

*The *Explorer Race* series, the *Shamanic Secrets* series and the *Ancient Secrets of Feminine Science* series.

ACKNOWLEDGEMENTS

When you write a book, it may seem like a solo effort, but there is an enormous amount of input you receive as you formulate the idea for the book, during the process of writing and afterward from all those friends who took the time to read the manuscript and send back corrections and suggestions. I will start by thanking the many authors whose books I have read over the years and who have given me inspiration. In the early days, this included Brad Steiger, Dick Sutphen, Ruth Montgomery and Dr. Edith Fiore. Later, about ten years ago, Robert Shapiro's inspirational books recommended seeking out benevolent experiences, benevolent companions and benevolent outcomes, and so I took his advice. I now count Robert as one of my good friends.

Next I would like to thank all of the people who contributed stories for this book. I kept their privacy by using only first names. I would like to thank all of you so much for sharing your stories of how requesting benevolent outcomes worked for you.

Thanks to the friends who read my manuscript, gave me suggestions and corrected my grammatical mistakes. As this includes people whose stories are included here, I won't name you but would just like to express my sincere appreciation for your taking the time to go through this line by line.

A special thanks to my wife, Dena, and daughter, Shannon, who both suggested that I have specific writing days instead of working on our normal entertainment distribution business. I would still be trying to find the time to write if not for having those days each week devoted to writing. And thanks to my son, Todd, who kept my computer up to date.

Finally, thanks to my publisher, Melody Swanson, who put my book on her "fast track," so that it is being released months before most books that go through this process.

THE GENTLE WAY
TABLE OF CONTENTS

PREFACE

When I'm browsing the shelves in a bookstore or even when I'm online on the Internet, I'll pick up one or more books whose title intrigues me. I will read the cover and a few pages in the front to see if the book has enough interesting subjects to be worth me purchasing it. So if you're doing the same thing now, let me explain what I believe you'll achieve from reading this self-help book:

1. This book will put you back in touch with your guardian angel or strengthen and expand the connection that perhaps you already have.
2. It will strengthen your spiritual beliefs.
3. You will have more fun and less stress in your life.
4. You will greatly lower the "fear factor" in everyday living.
5. In lowering the fear factor, this book will give you the confidence that you can travel in safety wherever you go, whether it is to work and back home, to the store, across the country or around the world.
6. It will assist you in achieving whatever goals you have set for yourself in your life.
7. This book will assist in finding just the right job for you.

8. It will even help you find that special person to share your life with.

9. It will assist you in handling those major challenges we all experience in life.

10. This book will even inspire you to learn more about our world and universe.

How can I promise all these benefits? It's because I have been using these concepts for over ten years, and I can report these successes from *direct knowledge and experience.* But this is a self-help guide, so that means it requires active participation on your part. What you are going to read in this book is *unique information* that you have *never seen before!* This book is for all faiths and beliefs, with the only requirement being a basic belief in angels.

At this point, if none of the above benefits has resonated with you, then it is time to return this book to the shelf and continue your search. I do request a *most benevolent outcome* that you will find the above intriguing enough to purchase the book and that it will enrich your life even more than you can imagine or anticipate. You'll discover what that means in the following pages.

CHAPTER ONE

ANGELS

The first goal of this book is to put you back in touch with that angelic being who watches over you during your life—your guardian angel—or to strengthen and expand the connection that you may already have. Then I want you to discover how much assistance you can receive in your life. First, let's begin with the usual way we view our relationship with our guardian angel.

Recently I was in Los Angeles on business and saw a friend from Montreal. In catching up on what the other had been doing, I mentioned that I was writing this book. My friend, Alphonse, said, "Tom, you've got to interview me for your book. Have I got some stories for you!" As you read what he related to me, notice the common theme of peril in each of the stories.

ENCOUNTERS WITH A GUARDIAN ANGEL

When Alphonse was three or four years old in Italy, there was a third-story window in the stairwell of his apartment house and he kept thinking that he could jump out of it. The day he decided to jump, he crouched down to leap off when suddenly a strange man in a suit grabbed him, preventing his fall and injury. He had never seen him before nor did he ever see him again.

At the age of nine, Alphonse was an immigrant on a ship to Canada with his family. The seas were rough, making the wooden deck slick from the waves. One pitch-black night, he found a hatch door open, went outside and immediately slipped on the rolling deck. He slid down under the rope sailors held on to as they made their way from one end of the ship to the other, hitting the plate at the edge of the deck. There was no place to hang on, and he was in danger of being tossed over the plate into the sea. Another passenger appeared out of nowhere and, by holding on to the deck rope, grabbed Alphonse and pulled him back to safety.

While driving in Canada one early winter, Alphonse, who never buckled his seat belt, suddenly heard a voice telling him to put the seat belt on. Two hundred yards later, he hit a patch of ice and slid into the V-section of a guardrail that bent the car in half. The impact broke his ribs as the seat belt held him from being thrown through the side window. After that, six other cars hit the same patch of ice and slid into his car in a multicar pileup.

On another occasion, Alphonse was working, planting posts at his country place with a large friend assisting him. The friend was on top of a ladder banging in the posts with a large splitter ax—one end was an ax and the other a sledgehammer. Alphonse was holding the posts, when suddenly he was told by a voice to move to the side. The splitter ax slipped out of his friend's hands and went into the ground right past where Alphonse was standing. It would have been sudden death had he remained in that position.

Several years ago in early August, Alphonse was participating in some summer skiing high in the mountains on the Italian-German border. He went off the trail out of bounds because the snow was better there. Suddenly his ski came off for no reason. After picking himself up, he saw a hole in the snow about five or six feet away, and through the hole he could see the village far below. Had he skied any farther, he would have gone off the cliff.

This past year, Alphonse completely totaled his car in another wreck, when he was forced into a pole by another car. He had his seat belt on, but the air bag did not deploy. The first person on the scene was an off-duty ambulance attendant. Alphonse had absolutely no injuries, but he was sure that his guardian angel had sent the attendant along just in case. I think another possibility was that his guardian angel was telling him to drive more conservatively or the next time an ambulance would be needed.

The theme of all these stories was that, yes, Alphonse has a guardian angel who does look after him and does his or her best to keep him from injury or death. Listening to one's guardian angel and acting on that seems almost instinctive. This occurred time after time for Alphonse and perhaps for many of you reading this.

MY GUARDIAN ANGEL HAS WORKED OVERTIME!

Back in my younger days, after leaving the army, my first successful business was operating a snow ski club for single adults in Dallas, Texas. During my days at TCU, I was chairman of the all-university trip committee and learned to ski on school trips. I started the ski club with virtually no money and bought an old school bus with a loan on my car in order to carry the club members up to the mountains in New Mexico every weekend during the ski season. I was so poor that I could not afford any insurance on the bus. I hoped that if we were ever in a wreck, I would be the first to die, as any injury lawsuits would mean I would be forever in debt.

On one of the first trips we took to New Mexico, the local ABC-affiliate TV station sent a news team with us. My guardian angel was looking out for me as we encountered a blizzard so bad that I could see only the markers beside the highway as I drove the bus. The engine's carburetor started freezing up, and we finally came to a stop with the front of the bus in New Mexico and the rear end in Texas (which could lead to some Texas jokes). We used the cameraman's lights to warm up the carburetor so that the bus could limp into the next town. The normal twelve-hour trip took twenty-two hours. We never had a news crew go with us again!

During another ski trip, the brake system for the bus went out in the middle of the night on our way back to Dallas. I drove the last two hundred miles with a guy pulling on the hand brake to slow us down as we went through small Texas towns. In one of those towns, he didn't quite slow us down enough, and I went around a 90-degree turn on two wheels. On subsequent New Mexico trips, we lost a gearbox driving down the mountain in Santa Fe and lost our electrical system heading back from Ruidoso, both potentially disastrous events. My guardian angel was working overtime!

GUARDIAN ANGELS IN YOUR DAILY LIFE

This is about the extent of what most people think about when guardian angels are mentioned. You don't think about them in your normal daily life, only in times of crisis. That's what we are about to change.

For the purposes of this book, we are going to use the commonly accepted belief that a guardian angel is an angelic being who has been assigned or volunteers to watch over you during your complete lifetime. The guardian angel is assisted by angelic guides who might be departed parents, relatives, friends or specialists in your field of work.

This book is a self-help guide for learning how to be in touch with your guardian angel on a daily basis and the huge benefits that will result. After reading this book, you may wish to read more about angels, and there are certainly many, many books about angels and others in the spiritual realm.

The Gentle Way is an easier path in life that you can take. I'm not going to prove this to you; you are going to prove it to yourself through direct experience. In the next chapter, I will explain how I discovered this simple system that I've been using for the past ten years in my work and personal life.

CHAPTER TWO

HOW I BEGAN

L earning how to be in touch with your guardian angel is truly a simple process. Making it part of your daily routine is the hardest part, for we are all creatures of habit. Adding something new to our daily lives, even though it might be highly beneficial, takes some work.

DISCOVERING BENEVOLENCE

I read a lot: business publications related to the entertainment industry (where I make my living) and many other types of books, especially those concerned with spiritual subjects. About ten years ago, I kept noticing that many of the spiritual books I was reading kept using the word "benevolent" to describe suggestions from the angelic realm. Robert Shapiro, in his inspirational book, *The Council of Creators* (from the *Explorer Race* series), wrote: ". . . seek out more benevolent experiences for yourself. Seek out more benevolent companions and experiences of benevolence for you and your companion or your family or your people." These suggestions seemed a little vague, but I was intrigued.

Benevolent (pronounced *be-nev-o-lent*) is not a commonly used word in everyday language, so it was quite noticeable to me. *Webster's Dictionary* defines the word benevolent as: "A kindly disposition to promote happiness and prosperity through good works, or by generosity in and pleasure of doing good works." I wasn't exactly sure how that related to what I was reading, but my curiosity was aroused.

ON TO BENEVOLENT OUTCOMES

Then I read a suggestion in Robert Shapiro's book to request a benevolent outcome for a specific need.* That sounded interesting, so I decided to try it. I realized that in order to see if my "experiment" worked, I would have to have some immediate feedback. Therefore, I began by requesting out loud a benevolent outcome for finding a parking place next to where I went daily to pick up my mail. There is limited parking there, which is not helped by having a busy veterinarian's office next door and a fast-food restaurant next to the veterinarian.

It worked fantastically well! Someone would pull out of a parking space just seconds before I arrived. I also tried this out when we went to the theater and when we went out for dinner. It worked again and again, with the only exceptions occurring when I was reluctant to pass by a parking space a little farther away. Then, as we walked up to the door of the restaurant or theater, I would see the vacant parking space waiting for me had I chosen to continue to drive closer to the entrance.

HOW DO BENEVOLENT OUTCOMES WORK?

I gradually expanded these requests to every phase of my life—business and personal—with the same success. In the

---

*I interchangeably use the words "benevolent outcome," "most benevolent outcome" and the abbreviation "MBO" throughout this book. These terms all mean and refer to the same thing.

following chapters, I will give you many examples of how to request these benevolent outcomes in your life, but let's begin with some basics:

* A request for a benevolent outcome is a request to your guardian angel for assistance.
* A request for a benevolent outcome has to be for exact intentions. You are asking for something specific.
* It can only be used benevolently, even if it is accidentally (or otherwise) said in some way that isn't benevolent.
* A benevolent outcome must be a request for something you wish to happen, not something you don't wish to occur.
* It will only work if the experience is benevolent for everyone, including those who cooperate consciously or on a subconscious level in bringing about your request.
* The request has to be for *you*, although others with you may be benevolently affected too.

Again, a request for a benevolent outcome is not just words you say; it is a *request of assistance* from your guardian angel. There are times when you can even feel energy after your request—I think that is a feedback of love from your guardian angel. Putting emotion and feeling into the request also helps. You are asking for a specific connection with a person or persons that encourages those people to do something they might otherwise do anyway, but your request asks them to do it at a specific time if it is not against their will or best interests.

You must request benevolent outcomes for positive results. As an example, you would say: "I request a most benevolent outcome for my drive to the office this morning."

You wouldn't say: "I request an MBO for not having a wreck on my drive to the office."

YOU CAN MAKE UNLIMITED REQUESTS

There is no limit to the number of requests you can make during your lifetime. You will not go "over quota." If you can, imagine enormous stacks of forms all around you, each one saying: "I request a most benevolent outcome for _____." The rest is blank and ready for you to fill in your request, so you fill in the blank and say "Thank you!" I estimate that I have requested at least *ten to fifteen thousand* benevolent outcomes over more than ten years, and I still have that huge mound of forms that will never diminish in size.

COMMON RESISTANCE TO REQUESTING BENEVOLENT OUTCOMES

As I have enthusiastically spread the word about requesting benevolent outcomes, I have encountered resistance for a couple of reasons. First, saying these requests sounds a little "weird," as most people do not use the word "benevolent" in everyday speech. I understand that. But this is "angel speech." So when you want your angel to listen to your request, you use their words.

Let's say one together so that you will start feeling more comfortable about using these words. I want you to say out loud right now:

Most Benevolent Outcome

"I request a most benevolent outcome for reading this book, and may the benefits be even more than I expect or can anticipate. Thank you."

That last half of the request is something additional that I will explain later. Have you said it yet? If you are in public, you can whisper it or you can physically write it, but it has to be done physically, not just by mentally thinking it.

Another resistance I have encountered is, "Oh, I'm not worthy of asking for assistance," or words to that effect. Who says you're not worthy? This is your own personal guardian angel you're speaking to. Some people have been verbally abused in life. Perhaps it was your parents or relatives who continually put you down. Possibly at school you had a teacher or teachers who did not know how to instill knowledge without berating you or belittling your efforts. Or perhaps you got that message in your religious institution. Whatever your situation, you have the right to speak to your very best friend in life—your guardian angel. Don't let anyone deny you that right.

I am also asked, "Tom, shouldn't we just ask for the important things in life and not the everyday small things?" My answer is, you have to ask for the small things in order to remember to ask for the important outcomes. Right now most of you are pretty disconnected from your guardian angel and guides. By requesting small things like a parking space or a seat on a subway or bus, you get immediate feedback that there is someone there. It gives you confidence to request the bigger results.

Make Requesting Benevolent Outcomes a Habit

Another important point to remember is that your guardian angel does not have vocal cords to respond to you. He or she responds by whispering messages and creating events that let you know you're never alone—he or she is always with you. When you request benevolent outcomes, you raise your awareness to these messages and events. It takes practice. If you only contact your guardian angel and guides in times of crisis, they can be slow to react because they have to figure out how to communicate with you. The more you request benevolent outcomes, the more "tuned in" you will be with your own guardian angel and guides.

That's why you must make requesting benevolent outcomes a habit. My French teacher taught me long ago that it takes a minimum of seven times repeating something before you learn it. I suggest putting up a small sign in your bathroom or on the refrigerator (or both) that says, "Request Benevolent Outcomes Today!" so that you'll remember. Otherwise the words in this book will slowly fade away as you are caught up in your daily activities.

YOUR GUARDIAN ANGEL IS YOUR BEST FRIEND

I am also asked, "Shouldn't I have my clergy person request these benevolent outcomes for me?" Can you imagine on a practical level even three hundred people calling their spiritual adviser all day long to ask him or her for a parking space, or about a meeting they are about to have, or any of the thousands of requests that those three hundred people would have during a given week? It would be overwhelmingly impossible.

You have to ask yourself: If you were moving and needed help, would you call someone and ask him or her to call your best friend to assist you in moving? Of course not. You would pick up the phone and call your friend and directly ask him or her to help you move. This is the same premise. You are requesting help from your guardian angel who is your very best friend.

Your guardian angel is there to assist you every minute of the day, but you have to ask. We can use the metaphor of your guardian angel and angelic guides sitting around watching a TV set of your life as you live it. They are pretty bored, because they don't get to help you very often. They can only "whisper in your ear," and most of the time you don't listen to them. They jump with joy when you acknowledge their presence and request even a little assistance. Requesting benevolent outcomes will strengthen your spiritual beliefs, because you will be receiving constant feedback that there are angelic beings who love you and wish to help you lead a more gentle, less stressful life—the Gentle Way!

This Is for You Personally

I have been asked if one can request a benevolent outcome for world peace, for victims of disasters and other such requests. The answer I received in my meditations is that the angelic beings who bring about benevolent outcomes are not the same as the ones who handle requests for other people.

Any time you include another person in your request or request something that is for other people, this is said in a different way, which I will devote a chapter to in this book. Both are quite similar but different. Requesting benevolent outcomes is for you personally.

In the following chapters, I will give my suggestions on all sorts of ways to request benevolent outcomes in your daily life. I suggest that you read this book over the course of a week. It will give you a chance to digest the many times you can request benevolent outcomes without all of them blending together or, to use a colloquial expression, "coming out your ears."

But I do wish to touch on one point before we move on. I did not invent talking to angels. This has been going on for thousands of years. I'm just showing you how you can do it in the twenty-first century. I simply tried out some obscure concepts and they worked, and now I am passing along my successes to you. Soon you'll be having many success stories of your own.

CHAPTER THREE

EASY STEPS

W e're going to begin with easy requests so that you will receive immediate feedback that requesting benevolent outcomes does work.

FINDING PARKING SPOTS AND SEATS

Not so long ago on a visit back to Sedona, Arizona (considered one of the most beautiful places in the United States), my wife, friends and I drove to the "uptown" section of Sedona for Mexican food. For many of you who have visited Sedona, you know that the parking there can be quite problematic because of the many gift shops and restaurants, divided by a busy four-lane street. I requested a most benevolent outcome when we left the hotel for a parking space in front of the restaurant. Every single parking space on both sides of the street was taken until we reached the restaurant. There, right at the front entrance, was "our" parking space. Again, this was immediate feedback that I received.

As an easy-to-do exercise, let's begin with the above example. Say you're going to a shopping center, dinner or a movie at a location where it is typically hard to find a parking space.

Say out loud (well before you arrive):

Most Benevolent Outcome

> "I request a most benevolent outcome for finding a parking space near _____. Thank you."

Now, I have had some friends say, "But, Tom, I use my 'parking angel' already." Here is why I think requesting a benevolent outcome is better. If you just request the nearest parking space, your angel or guide will comply, but that might not be the most benevolent place to have your car parked. Someone could open a car door too hard and ding the side of your car. Or someone might back into your car and dent it. By being too close, you might miss that old friend of yours you haven't seen in ages or the sale you wouldn't have known about had you not walked past it on the way to your destination.

But requesting a benevolent outcome works perfectly! It might seem initially that it didn't, until you realize all the other possibilities that come into play. Ninety-nine percent of the time you'll be close, and when you aren't, you'll know there must be a good reason. Plus, we are working toward you making a habit out of requesting benevolent outcomes. Finding a parking place is a constant problem for many people, so it's a perfect exercise.

Clara in Seattle emailed to tell me that the first time she requested a benevolent outcome was to pick up her grandson on a hot summer day. She knew she would have to wait for him and hoped to find a space up close. She requested an MBO (my abbreviation for most benevolent outcome). Arriving at the school, the only space available was in the last row, but it was the only one in the shade of a tree! It made a believer out of Clara, who says she requests MBOs for everything. She says it has never failed her.

As part of my film distribution business, my wife and I go to press screenings of movies all the time. I like to sit in the very middle of the row, preferably halfway up, so that the very center of the screen is in my line of sight. I always request a benevolent outcome for having those seats available when we arrive in the theater, and invariably, they are.

Those of you who commute to and from work by train, subway or bus may find it difficult to find a seat. Then you should say out loud:

> ❧ Most Benevolent Outcome ❧
>
> "I request a most benevolent outcome for having a seat on the _____ [train, bus, subway, etc.] when I board. Thank you."

Not too long ago, I was in Paris. A friend and I had to go across to the other side of the city on business. We had to take three connecting subways on the way there and two to return, so I requested an MBO for a seat on each one. As we boarded, there was a seat waiting for me, even though it was a busy time of day.

For Misplaced Items and When Buying a Home

Here are some more easy-to-use examples: Any time we misplace something in our house, we request a benevolent outcome for finding it, and it always turns up. Two of our friends, Don and Karen, recently moved to San Diego to be close to their children and new grandchild. As you know, when you move you have a bunch of boxes and it's difficult to remember everything you put in them. Karen had that same situation with numerous boxes in her garage. She needed some important papers for the bank but couldn't recall which box they were in. She requested a benevolent outcome for finding the right box, and in the first box she chose, there were the papers right on top!

Just the other day, we needed to find a warranty on our digital camera to have it repaired. My daughter and wife searched through the box we normally keep the warranties in but couldn't find it, so they searched everywhere else. The camera store claimed they had no record of us even buying the camera. Finally, my daughter said:

Most Benevolent Outcome

"I request a most benevolent outcome for finding the camera warranty paper."

Then she went through the same box again. There it was, just a little hidden!

Two of our friends, Joy and Bob, purchased a home in the country. Every time they have closed on a house in the past, they experienced problems at the closing—mistakes in the paperwork and so on. This time they requested a most benevolent outcome for the closing and reported that they sailed through the process with no problems.

CAR TROUBLE

During the month of August, my wife, some friends and I drove to Mena, Arkansas, for the weekend. On the drive over, I discovered that my van was short on coolant for the air conditioner. Not having sufficient cooling in the final dog days of summer in the South can be miserable, so I requested a most benevolent outcome for getting it repaired. The motel told me that finding a place open on Saturday in such a small town might not be possible, but they gave me the name of a tire store nearby to try.

We were there at 7:00 A.M. the next morning, but it would not open until 8:00 A.M. I was drawn to a service station that was open nearby and asked if they knew of a garage to service the air conditioner. A young man who "just happened" to be there suggested an automotive repair garage several blocks away and recited the phone number from memory. Finding the garage closed, we returned to the tire store, and I said:

> *Most Benevolent Outcome*
>
> "I request a most benevolent outcome to have the air conditioner serviced today [say this with feeling]! Thank you."

The lady said that they didn't have the equipment, so I pulled out the telephone number I had kept and asked her to telephone them.

The garage owner answered and said that normally he did not work on Saturday, but to come by, as he was repairing a UPS truck we had seen in the driveway. He replenished the coolant and charged me only one-third of what I would have paid in Dallas. And as a side benefit, we were able to view his unbelievable collection of old Indian motorcycles, a 1942 Hudson sedan, a marble collection and toy cars in their original boxes. He had taught automotive repair at a local college for twenty-five years before retiring. Had the lady who knew him not telephoned, he might not have said yes to us. And it's obvious to me that it was no coincidence that the young man was there at that service station to suggest we try the repair garage—my guardian angel arranged that!

WHEN TRAVELING

Here's another example: Several years ago, my son and I, along with his friend Jason and Jason's father, flew to Salt Lake

City, Utah, and camped all the way up to Yellowstone National Park and back. What a wonderful trip! I knew that our flight back to Dallas was oversold, so I volunteered the four of us to be "bumped." Typically, the airline compensates with free tickets or coupons to use in purchasing tickets, which I thought we could use the next year. Naturally, I requested a most benevolent outcome. They did not need our seats, but for volunteering, they gave us four first-class seats. My son, his friend and his friend's dad had never flown first class, so this was the treat of their lives. The following summer, our schedules did not coincide and we were not able to return—therefore making the memories of this trip more special with all the benevolent outcomes shared with friends.

Two years ago, I went to Saint Petersburg, Russia, on business, and the company I was visiting informed me that they would have to put me in a smaller hotel. All the larger ones were sold out because Paul McCartney would be performing in concert. Upon arrival, I asked to be taken to the ticket office, as I had never had the chance to see him in a live performance. This was the day before the concert, so the odds of getting a ticket were not too good.

Naturally I said:

> *Most Benevolent Outcome*
>
> *"I request a most benevolent outcome for buying a ticket as close to the front as possible. Thank you."*

They had one ticket left in the first forty or so rows, and I wound up sitting right of center in Row 27. This concert was the first ever to be performed in front of the famous Hermitage Museum that I had visited earlier that day. What an experience!

One night, our two friends, Bob and Mary, were driving back from an Alanis Morissette concert in Fort Worth, about thirty miles from Dallas. It was late, and Mary requested a benevolent outcome for their drive back home. They stopped at a stop sign in the middle of the highway, almost at the top of a hill; the stop sign was very hard to see in the dark. They heard a loud squeal as a truck came up behind them, slammed on its brakes and skidded sideways, narrowly missing them. She stated, "It was an MBO for sure!"

FOR CONCERT TICKETS AND RAFFLES

When the American Airlines Center opened in Dallas, the first concert there was the Eagles. I had always wanted to see them but had been out of town when the tickets went on sale, and they had immediately sold out. I told my wife that we should take a chance and requested a most benevolent outcome for buying two good tickets. I told her to wait for me on the front steps of the Center while I tried to see if I could buy tickets from a scalper or someone who had two extra tickets.

There were almost no tickets available, and those that were available were priced too high. But I have such confidence in requesting MBOs that I just *knew* that I would find two somehow. Suddenly, a guy just passing by saw my two fingers raised and told me that he had heard there were some tickets left at the box office. I thanked him and went and found my wife, and we went over to the ticket window where I bought two of the last four seats they had left to sell, eighteen rows from the stage. Obviously, my guardian angel arranged for that passing gentleman to inform me about the tickets. That's the way requesting benevolent outcomes works.

My son returned from an all-night high school graduation party with a Sony PlayStation he had won in a drawing.

Although it was the second largest prize, it was the one he really wanted. He explained to me that he had requested a benevolent outcome "two times." He was a little anxious, as once was really enough!

THE IMPOSSIBLE IS OBTAINABLE!

Now my son is in college, and he took a computer course last summer. He was busy studying for a final and could not drive down to Waco to drop off a videotape of a PowerPoint sales presentation, so my wife and I jumped in the car and drove down the hundred miles to his college. I requested a benevolent outcome for the drive down but was dreading the drive back because I knew we would be hitting the Dallas drive-home traffic around 5:00 P.M. As we started our return, my wife said:

Most Benevolent Outcome

"Well, I request a most benevolent outcome that we will see little traffic on our drive."

I thought, "Oh sure, lots of luck—the traffic is just going to disappear!"

Well, we sailed through the freeways around downtown like it was midday. We actually arrived back home in better time than the drive down had taken. In a meditation afterward, I asked about that and was told that we should ask for the impossible, because it will actually exceed anything we can think of as a resolution.

C.J. in Wisconsin emailed to tell me that after she left her job, it had started to snow and the roads were "getting nasty." So she requested a most benevolent outcome that the roads would clear and she would arrive home safely. She reported that the "roads kept getting clearer and clearer . . . too cool! I love this stuff!"

That's why I had you say in the last chapter: ". . . and may the benefits be even more than I expect or can anticipate." You have to be spontaneous in saying this, almost as an afterthought. You want to be surprised at how good the outcome really turns out to be—more than you could have imagined. Your guardian angel and guides will have you laughing and saying, "I didn't even think of that!" This was something I learned after requesting benevolent outcomes for a long time, and I am still surprised and sometimes amazed at the results of this request.

My friend Robert told me that one time he was to meet his friend Wendy across town and he requested a benevolent outcome to arrive on time. When he encountered a traffic jam on a large highway interchange, he doubted that it was working. He called Wendy and she informed him that she was behind schedule and hadn't left her house yet. After hanging up, he suddenly had the "inspiration" to exit and go pick up some mail—he'd had been meaning to get to it for two weeks but had not had the time. After quickly picking up the mail, he returned to the freeway, which was now clear. He still arrived before his friend Wendy. He says that this was a "gift." Notice that he listened to his guardian angel.

REQUESTING MBOs IS AN EXPANSION OF WHAT YOU'VE BEEN DOING

Some of you reading this book may already have had experiences in requesting outcomes on a more mental or subjective level. My wife and I attended a seminar on an Alaskan cruise recently where I was allowed to introduce MBOs. Two ladies came up to me afterward with their own stories that they felt were benevolent outcomes. First, Joan from Vancouver related how she and a friend had been on a previous trip to Alaska and her friend had really wanted to see a bear. So Joan requested a "divine order," and a bear appeared right on the trail they had taken into the forest.

Lena, from Perth, Australia, was telephoned by a friend, who lived thirty minutes farther than her out of town, to ask for a ride to see a well-known speaker. She didn't mind picking the friend up but did not relish the thought of driving in the late hours after the program out of the city limits to drop the friend off and then back another thirty minutes to her house. She really wished that somehow she would not have to make that drive. Out of the blue, a couple called who lived near the friend and said that they could take her back with them. Lena was positive that this was a benevolent outcome when she related this story to me.

In my meditation, the message I received is that you should continue with these requests. But requesting benevolent outcomes is an expansion of what you have been doing, as it gives it structure and it becomes a habit instead of something you think to do occasionally. Requests for benevolent outcomes are to be said out loud—you can whisper or write them if need be. This is a physical world, and you want a physical action to take place. Therefore, you must request the benevolent outcome in a physical manner by writing it or saying the request out loud.

THANK YOUR GUARDIAN ANGEL

When you see the positive results from requesting benevolent outcomes, be sure to thank your guardian angel. I say, "Thank you, thank you, thank you," and I don't say that to anyone else. Three thank-yous are just for my angel.

All of the above stories should not only provide you with some idea of what to request benevolent outcomes for in your life, but you should be able to see how doing this lowered the stress and increased the "fun factor" for myself, my family and my friends who request benevolent outcomes on a daily basis. In the following chapters, I will give you many more suggestions and success stories, but you can start experimenting with these requests right now!

Easy Steps for Requesting MBOs: A Quick Review

* Request the benevolent outcomes out loud, whispered or in writing.
* Start with easy requests for immediate feedback.
* Be very specific with your request.
* Make requesting benevolent outcomes a habit.
* Requesting a benevolent outcome with emotion and feeling reinforces the request.
* Don't be afraid to ask for the impossible.
* You can request that the outcome be even more than you can expect or imagine.
* Thank your guardian angel for fulfilling your request.

CHAPTER FOUR

HOME LIFE

Τ his is a topic that everyone will want information on: how to use these requests for benevolent outcomes in your home life.

MAKING LIFE DECISIONS

Let's begin with young adults in their late teens and early twenties. Say you're graduating from high school soon, and you have that big question of what to do with your life. Do you go to college, and if so, which one? Do you attend a trade school, or should you join the military? Or should you attempt to find a job somewhere while you try and sort all this out?

I suggest you say:

Most Benevolent Outcome

> *"I request a most benevolent outcome for choosing the best course in life for me to grow and which will lead me to a productive life. Thank you."*

You can change this request to better reflect your particular circumstances.

If you're a parent or guardian, you want these young men and women to succeed in life just as much if not more than you have, having had years of "on-the-job training" in your own personal life. I suggest you say:

> *Most Benevolent Outcome*
>
> *"I request a most benevolent outcome for my assistance and guidance of _____ [say his or her name] to make the best choice that will result in his or her growth and him or her becoming a productive member of society. Thank you."*

Just remember that what you think your children should be doing and what they are led to do may be two different things. You can only guide them so far, and then they have to fly on their own. Please support them, even if you feel that what they are doing is a mistake. Mistakes are great teachers, and in many instances they may help your children to mature and grow much faster than they would have otherwise.

REGARDING YOUR HOUSE

For you young adults, you will eventually need to find your own place to live. It will probably be an apartment, or it could be a room until you are able to afford better accommodations. You should say:

> *Most Benevolent Outcome*
>
> *"I request a most benevolent outcome for finding a place to live that will be within my budget, be safe and secure, have good neighbors and be even better than I can hope for or expect. Thank you."*

You can say something similar if you are in the market to purchase a house. Say:

> *Most Benevolent Outcome*
>
> "I request a most benevolent outcome to find a house that will be perfect for me and my family, that will be within our budget, that will have good neighbors and that will be even better than we can hope for or expect. Thank you."

And eventually when you sell that house, you might wish to state:

> *Most Benevolent Outcome*
>
> "I request a most benevolent outcome for finding the right real estate agent who will sell our house at the maximum price it will bring and that will be the most benevolent for us. Thank you."

When you buy that house, it may need a little or a lot of remodeling. My wife loves to remodel houses, so we have done several over the years. When she asks for bids for painting, construction, tiling, plumbing, electrical, heating/air conditioning or any other work on our house, she requests a benevolent outcome for finding the right company or individual to do the best work at the best price.

WHEN PURCHASING A CAR

Many of you will have to purchase an automobile or motorcycle for commuting to work. When you start your search, say:

> *Most Benevolent Outcome*
>
> "I request a most benevolent outcome for finding the best vehicle for my budget that will have the fewest mechanical problems during the time I own it and at a better price than I could expect or hope for. Thank you."

You may wish to keep this pretty general, as your guardian angel might find a car or cycle that is much better than you think you can afford.

When you are negotiating with the dealership or an individual, you may wish to say:

Most Benevolent Outcome

"*I request a most benevolent outcome in this negotiation or bargaining for me! Thank you.*"

This same request can be used for any item you have to buy or any service that does not have a set price.

MEDICAL CARE AND SCHOOL

What if you need to find a doctor or a dentist in the area you have moved to? Request a benevolent outcome for finding the right doctor or the right dentist for you who will be the most benevolent for your needs. You can structure the MBO request depending upon your circumstances and what you need at that time.

School is an important subject for all parents and guardians. From preschool all the way through high school, you will be taking an active part in making sure your child receives the best education possible. So you will need to request a most benevolent outcome in choosing that preschool, if you have a choice, and then MBOs each time you meet with teachers and counselors. When my wife and I had meetings with our children's teachers and counselors, we would always ask for a benevolent outcome. We never failed to reach an agreement that was in the best interest of our children.

There are an enormous number of school activities these days: football, basketball, baseball, volleyball, swimming, track and field, lacrosse, band, cheerleading, dance, debate clubs, foreign-language clubs, Cub Scouts, Boy Scouts, Girl Scouts, theater, video yearbooks, robotics clubs and many others too numerous to list here. If you are a parent involved in these activities, you can request a benevolent outcome each time you attend meetings and work with your children.

If you are a student involved with these activities, then you can request a most benevolent outcome each time you are in competition that you will do your very best and feel relaxed. You can also request benevolent outcomes each time you take a school test. Say:

Most Benevolent Outcome

"*I request a most benevolent outcome to recall all that I have studied and that I remain relaxed and confident during the test. Thank you.*"

Another stressful time for students is when they begin their studies in a new school. As a student you can say:

Most Benevolent Outcome

"*I request a most benevolent outcome in meeting good, honest people who will become my true friends. Thank you.*"

DATING AND SEXUAL ACTIVITY

When you start dating, you might say:

Most Benevolent Outcome

"*I request a most benevolent outcome for an enjoyable, safe time with my date. Thank you.*"

And at whatever age you decide to become sexually active, you can say:

> *Most Benevolent Outcome*
>
> *"I request a most benevolent outcome that I remain safe and disease free with my sexual partner. Thank you."*

Naturally you can name that person in the above request, should you so desire.

If you are a woman, you may wish to add: ". . . and that I will only become pregnant when I wish to and with the man who will love and nurture our child forever." For a man, you may wish to add: ". . . and that I will only father a child with a woman I love and wish to spend the rest of my life with."

FINDING WHAT'S BEEN LOST

As a parent or guardian, when you are out shopping, going to amusement parks or doing other things with your young children, there is always the possibility that they might become lost. You are in a panic stage when this occurs. Should this ever happen, stop and immediately say:

> *Most Benevolent Outcome*
>
> *"I request a most benevolent outcome for the safe return of my child now! Thank you."*

Terry emailed to tell me that she and her daughter had gone to a swap meet at their school stadium. She thought she lost her wallet there and returned with her daughter, while asking for a benevolent outcome in finding it. One immediate benefit that resulted was her and her daughter both buying something that they hadn't seen when they had previously strolled through the area. Then later she found the wallet between the cushions on the sofa at home. "It was incredible," she remarked.

My whole family went to see one of the first Harry Potter movies not too long ago, and upon our return, I discovered that my wedding ring was not on my finger. I had lost my first wedding ring in the river rapids during a canoe trip with my son's Boy Scout troop, so I was not too pleased with the thought of purchasing another one. I looked all over the kitchen counter and floor, and then thought I might have lost it during an exciting scene in the movie, so I called the manager of the theater to ask him to search for it. No ring.

I decided that it was time to request an MBO to find the ring (which I should have done earlier). The important thing was, *I released* the stress I was feeling about the loss. My wife went upstairs and found my ring next to the sink, where in the rush to leave for the movie, it had slipped off when I had quickly washed my hands with soap.

YOUR PETS

When you are looking for a pet for you and/or your family, you can say:

Most Benevolent Outcome

"I request a most benevolent outcome in finding just the right pet for us. Thank you."

Pets sometimes do get themselves lost. If we are careless in leaving the gate open, our dog, Sandy, loves to explore the neighborhood. One summer day, unbeknownst to me, our gardeners had arrived to mow our lawn and my wife had opened the gate. I let Sandy out, and as she shot out of the gate, I yelled for our gardeners to catch her, but she would have none of that. I quickly requested an MBO for her safe return. She crossed the busy four-lane street we live on without being hit by any cars. I followed and cornered her in the alley with the help of my gardener.

The other night our back gate (which had just had its electric motor replaced) mysteriously opened by itself. Once again, Sandy was gone. When she goes out the back, she normally heads down the alley to where some hunting dogs are kept to say hello before moving on. I was resigned to searching for her in the dark—and it was cold out! I got in my car to drive down the alley and again quickly requested an MBO for her safe return. I had barely driven out of our driveway when there she was in my head-lights in the next-door neighbor's driveway. I opened my car door and in she jumped—she just loves to take trips in the car.

One lady I know recently recounted how her cat was in distress, so she took her cat to the veterinarian and requested a MBO that the cat would be okay. It turned out to be an easy problem to treat. Liberally request benevolent outcomes for all phases of your life with your loving animal. They are here to teach you something. Treat them gently.

IN YOUR SEARCH FOR ENLIGHTENMENT

Keeping in mind that this book is for all religious faiths and beliefs, for many people, the search for a religious institution they can feel at home in can be a trying time, especially in a large city with many choices. You can request a benevolent outcome for finding the perfect group of people to worship with. You might say:

Most Benevolent Outcome

"I request a most benevolent outcome for finding the perfect place to worship for me and my family that will result in our spiritual growth. Thank you."

You can also ask for a general MBO for yourself. I suggest you say:

> *Most Benevolent Outcome*
>
> *"I request a most benevolent outcome that I be enlightened in such a way in this life that I can be of the greatest benefit to those I meet as well as bring about comfort and peace to myself. Thank you!"*

You want to say these two above requests with a lot of feeling.

When Facing Surgery

As you go along in life, there may be one or more times when you must have an operation in a hospital. That's a really good time to request a benevolent outcome. I had to have orthoscopic surgery on my knee a couple of years ago to repair some cartilage damage from a ski injury and then later another surgery to repair a hernia, probably caused by carrying around seventy-pound trunks on my travels to film markets over the past twenty-four years.

I completely freed myself from stress and worry over the procedures by requesting benevolent outcomes for the surgeries. I remember that just before they put me to sleep in the operating room for the hernia surgery, I was wishing the surgeon and nurses a great and most benevolent day!

Funerals and Memorials

Some time in your life, you will attend a funeral or some type of memorial service for one of your friends or relatives. You can request a benevolent outcome to be able to give comfort to those who are grieving for the person who passed away.

Just recently my wife and I attended a memorial service for our friend Mary, who passed away within six months of being diagnosed with cancer. We ordered flowers to be sent to the church where the service was to be held. As we had never been to this church, on the Saturday morning of the service, I looked up the address on a map of the area. I noticed that there was another street with an almost identical name that ran parallel one block away. I telephoned the florist, who said that the flowers would be delivered just before the service, and I explained about the two similarly named streets. He said he would convey the information to the delivery driver. I requested a benevolent outcome for their arrival on time.

I stood at the doorway of the church until the very last second before the service began, but the flowers did not arrive. Perplexed, I went in and sat down for the service, wondering if they would bring them in at some point, but there was no break. After the service, I checked with the Assistant Reverend, and she said that they were delivered fifteen minutes after the service had begun. The delivery driver apologized, saying that he had been caught in traffic. I think he turned on the wrong street.

But what made this a *perfect* benevolent outcome was that our flowers were sitting in the middle of the long buffet table where all the food was placed. The flowers brightened up the table and brightened up the room! Trust in requesting benevolent outcomes. *They work perfectly!*

CHAPTER FIVE

THE CORPORATE ENVIRONMENT

For most of us, work takes up about one-third of our lives. Nothing can be more nerve-racking than applying for a job. I'm going to assume that if you are looking for a job, you have read all the books about applying for jobs at your skill level, how to prepare a resume, how to dress for the interview and the importance of being on time.

WHEN INTERVIEWING

When you begin contacting potential employers, you might say:

Most Benevolent Outcome

> "*I request a most benevolent outcome for being hired for the perfect position for my growth and expertise. Thank you.*"

And as you call the companies to ask for interviews, say:

Most Benevolent Outcome

> "*I request a most benevolent outcome for obtaining an interview with this company.*"

When you go in for your interview, say:

> *Most Benevolent Outcome*
>
> *"I request a most benevolent outcome for this interview. Thank you."*

Keep in mind that you have requested an MBO for the perfect job for *you*, so even if you are being turned down time after time, you have to understand that the perfect job will be coming. Perhaps someone else has to leave first, and your guardian angel is keeping abreast of when that will happen.

WHEN HIRING

On the other side of the table is the employer. You want to hire someone who will contribute and help your business to grow and be successful. Therefore, you say:

> *Most Benevolent Outcome*
>
> *"I request a most benevolent outcome to hire someone who will be perfect for this position and for my business. Thank you."*

When you advertise, you should say:

> *Most Benevolent Outcome*
>
> *"I request a most benevolent outcome that this advertisement reaches the person who is perfect for this job. Thank you."*

What will happen is that your angel will check with his or her counterparts and make sure that that perfect person reads the newspaper or Internet ad and so on that you have placed. Then listen to your intuition (your guardian angel) as you interview the applicants. You will have a definite feeling that this is the person for the job.

A SURPRISINGLY BENEVOLENT OUTCOME

My daughter worked for a major airline here in Dallas for three and a half years. After one year, employees can apply for any other position in the company, but at that time there was a hiring freeze because of 9/11. After they lifted the freeze, she applied for three other positions, and each time someone else— usually a supervisor—was given the position. Finally she was promoted to the customer-service division that took complaint calls all day long. A few months of that and she was ready to leave. This was a benevolent outcome as you'll see below.

Because our business had dramatically increased during that same time period, we badly needed someone to work in our company, and so we hired her on a full-time basis, paying her the same money she had been making working for the airline full-time *and* working with us part-time. It was not only a good move for her monetarily (she recently received a raise in pay), but now she also has the time to work on some ideas for creating her own business.

YOUR FIRST DAY ON THE JOB

On the first day in a new job, you often feel the pressure of "fitting in" and making new friends. Before entering your new workplace, you might wish to say:

Most Benevolent Outcome

"I request a most benevolent outcome for my first day at work, that it be enjoyable and that I find it easy to work with my new colleagues and make new friends. Thank you."

You may wish to change this to fit your circumstances.

Now let's cover some of the general positions in a company.

Sales

Sales—that's something I know a lot about. In my early years, after I left military service, I held a variety of sales jobs to put food on the table while I was starting my first tour business. I sold knives and keys on the road. I sold bad-debt collection plans, townhouses, pots and pans, insurance and newspaper advertisments. I learned something in every one of those jobs.

When you are about to make a presentation to a prospective client, say:

Most Benevolent Outcome

"I request a most benevolent outcome for this presentation for or meeting with this prospective client. Thank you."

If this is an important meeting with large ramifications for your company, you may wish to add to the above request, ". . . and may it be even better than I hope or can expect." As I mentioned previously, add that almost as an afterthought or spontaneously.

Even if you are in a phone room with three hundred other people trying to sell some product or service, you can request a benevolent outcome each morning (or whatever time your shift is) that you will be put in contact with people who will want to purchase something from you. It's the same situation if you must make "cold calls" all day long from business to business or house to house. Request an MBO each day that you will meet people who wish to buy from you.

Whether you are an insurance agent who receives leads from your company, work as a real estate agent, sell cars for an automotive dealership or are in one of the many sales positions for commission, you can say:

> *Most Benevolent Outcome*
>
> *"I request a most benevolent outcome that I meet those people who wish to purchase from me today. Thank you."*

You'll find that the percentage of sales you make will rise. You can adjust this request to fit your specific circumstances.

When I finished the first draft of this book, I gave it to several of my friends to read and make corrections and suggestions. My friend Gill in New York was the only person I sent the manuscript to whom I had not had a chance to teach how to request benevolent outcomes. Her husband is a real-estate agent, and as anyone in the business knows, you are constantly looking for houses to sell as the listing agent and then for prospective buyers. I suggested that she request an MBO that her husband would be successful in finding listings and selling.

She told me that the first morning she requested the benevolent outcome, her husband said he was going to see a lady about a listing. She asked if it looked promising, and he replied, "No, it doesn't, but I'll go anyway." She didn't tell him about the request, and they both left for work. That afternoon she did tell her two children what she had requested. When he arrived back home, he related to them, "You know, you wouldn't believe it! I not only got that listing, but another one walked into the office today!" She says it was "extraordinary."

Making a presentation internally in your company can be stressful if it is to higher management. So you might say:

> *Most Benevolent Outcome*
>
> *"I request a most benevolent outcome for my presentation, and may it be even better than I can hope or expect. Thank you."*

When you do this, your stress level will go down, as you will feel confident that you will do your best with the presentation.

ACCOUNTING AND
RESEARCH AND DEVELOPMENT

What about the accounting department? If the sales division is the right arm of the business, the accounting department is the kidneys, as everything has to flow through this department. As one of the accountants or the accountant of your company, perhaps you are not as appreciated as the other parts of the company, but are you important!

When you take part in meetings with management and other departments, you can request benevolent outcomes for those meetings, especially for those where you must make reports on the health of the company. And when you must prepare tax reports, you should request an MBO that you will sail through the report with no problems.

If you are in research and development, each day you may wish to say something like:

Most Benevolent Outcome

"I request a most benevolent outcome for being drawn to finding new products and uses of our products that will be beneficial to me and to my company. Thank you."

Change this to fit your circumstances.

PRODUCTION AND SECURITY

Most Benevolent Outcome

"I request a most benevolent outcome that I will work in safety throughout the day and that my relations with my coworkers, supervisors and managers will be enjoyable and appreciated. Thank you."

If your job entails work in the production of the product for your company, then as you arrive at the plant, you should say the above MBO. You can change it to fit your specific circumstances. Request MBOs for each of your production meetings.

If you work in security for your company, you may wish to say each day:

> *Most Benevolent Outcome*
>
> "*I request a most benevolent outcome for my safety and to keep my company safe and secure as well. Thank you.*"

You might be drawn to discovering one of the many types of spyware used by competing companies or other governments, or possibly by a person trying to smuggle out vital information.

MANAGEMENT AND NONPROFITS

As the manager or the head of the company, your responsibilities multiply. As you meet with your managers, supervisors and employees, request a benevolent outcome that the meetings are productive and will contribute to the success of the company. And naturally, request an MBO for those meetings with your clients, lawyers and government personnel.

If you work for a nonprofit organization raising money for a charity, each day state:

> *Most Benevolent Outcome*
>
> "*I request a most benevolent outcome to meet with generous individuals and companies who will respond to our need for funding. Thank you.*"

PROBLEMS AT WORK

So let's look at some of the problems you may encounter at work. Possibly you're having a problem just working with another person due to a personality conflict. You can request a benevolent outcome each time you must work with this person. If it is every minute of the day, then you can request the MBO at the start of the day. If you just meet with that person periodically, remember to request the MBO before the meeting so that it will go smoothly and without conflict.

But perhaps the person is just too nasty to work with, and you suffer verbal or sexual abuse and innuendo, so you know you absolutely must speak to your supervisor about the situation. Then you say:

Most Benevolent Outcome

"I request a most benevolent outcome for favorable results from my meeting with _____ [your supervisor]. Thank you."

No one has the right to treat you in this manner—not in this day and age.

We must also cover the really serious problem of discovering illegal activities either in your department or in your company. This may involve going all the way to meet with the head of the company or even with outside authorities. When you do, you may wish to say something like:

Most Benevolent Outcome

"I request a most benevolent outcome for my meeting with _____ [say the person's name] and revealing these improprieties in my company. Thank you."

Again, you may wish to adjust this request to fit your specific situation. Know that your guardian angel will take care of you and that whatever happens will be the best for you and your family!

A person who is conducting illegal activities is a liability to that company. His or her actions may cost the company millions of dollars in legal fees, settlements and lost revenue, affect the company's good name and cause the company's stock to plummet. Good people may quit because of that person's actions, weakening the company and putting it in danger of bankruptcy. Most managers will understand this and take appropriate action. If they don't, you may be the one to cost them the legal fees and settlement. Whatever happens, it will be a benevolent outcome for you!

CHAPTER SIX

SMALL BUSINESSES

I f you own a small business—from one to twenty employees, let's say—you are the "chief cook and bottle washer."
It may be the corner convenience store, a grocery store, a
retailer, a contractor business or one of many service companies. I'm not able to cover the many thousands of individual
businesses, but I'll attempt to be general enough to cover
many of them. You can request benevolent outcomes for
obtaining new business, negotiating contracts, hiring the best
employees for you, buying from the best vendors, working
with attorneys, filling out government tax forms or other
forms and so on.

FOR SOLICITING NEW CLIENTS AND NEGOTIATING CONTRACTS

Two friends of ours, Billy and Josephine, own a high-end
painting and contracting business. A couple of years ago, the
economy was down in this area and things had been tough for
them. Billy hadn't gotten used to requesting benevolent outcomes yet, but his wife Jo and I requested a benevolent outcome for their business to pick up. Within a month, they
landed a painting contract for a 20,000-square-foot house that
would take over a year to complete.

When you make a proposal to a potential new customer, say:

> *Most Benevolent Outcome*
>
> *"I request a most benevolent outcome for doing business with this company. Thank you."*

You can vary this statement according to the circumstances. You can also add spontaneously, if you think this might be a big deal for you, ". . . and may it be even better than I expect or can imagine."

I say something similar to this MBO request all the time when I am soliciting new clients. If I don't get the business, then I know that either I might have had more problems with that potential client than the business was worth, or that something even better is going to come our way.

I received an email from a lady in Iran who had struggled with her business there. After reading about requesting MBOs, she requested a benevolent outcome for her business to pick up. She reported that just in the past four days before emailing me, she'd signed four contracts, and it appeared she would sign four more the following week.

When I'm negotiating a contract, I will say:

> *Most Benevolent Outcome*
>
> *"I request a most benevolent outcome for the best agreement for our company. Thank you."*

In this way, I know that the terms will be the best that we can negotiate. Try and be more aware, and listen for insights and messages from your guardian angel. If you have a bad feeling about a contract, don't disregard it. Back off if you feel you must.

SECURITY AND SAFETY ISSUES

If you operate any type of retail establishment, then you know that shoplifting can drain your profits. Each day you can say:

Most Benevolent Outcome

> *"I request a most benevolent outcome that my store and employees remain safe and our goods secure from shoplifting. Thank you."*

Possibly what will occur is that a security person on duty will happen by just at the time a shoplifter will be about to pick up an item, or the shoplifter will be seen on one of the security cameras by your security people, or perhaps a policeman might stroll in at just the right time to prevent the theft. Request an MBO each day and see for yourself how those thefts go down. The above request works in the same way if there is a danger of being robbed at gunpoint.

If you are a contractor, then safety is a big issue for you. Injuries on the job are costly for you in terms of lost manpower, lost hours and insurance costs. So I suggest you say each day:

Most Benevolent Outcome

> *"I request a most benevolent outcome for my safety and the safety of my employees today, and that our work is highly productive. Thank you."*

Don't forget to request an MBO each time you and your crew drive to and from each job site.

EMPLOYEE ISSUES

While hiring the right employee in a large company is important, finding the right person for a job can make or break a small company. I always request an MBO for hiring the best person to fill a particular position in my company.

Some small business owners must hire illegal immigrants to fill positions that they can't find anyone else to perform. If those are your circumstances, whether this is a contracting, restaurant or service operation, you know that if they are deported, it can almost shut down your whole operation. You might wish to say each week, day or month:

> *Most Benevolent Outcome*
>
> *"I request a most benevolent outcome that my employees will be safe and are able to work for me as long as I need them. Thank you."*

I'm sure I don't have to remind you to treat them with respect and to pay them reasonable wages.

VENDORS AND FINANCING

If you or someone in your company has to constantly purchase goods from vendors, then you should say:

> *Most Benevolent Outcome*
>
> *"I request a most benevolent outcome for obtaining the best prices, the best quality and the best terms from my vendors. Thank you."*

You may find that your vendors suddenly offer you better prices and terms than you had before, even if you have not asked for them.

As a small business owner, there are times when you must find financing for your business to make it grow or to pay off short-term debts. You may need bank financing or investors.

When you meet with a banker, say:

> *Most Benevolent Outcome*
>
> *"I request a most benevolent outcome for obtaining the financing I need at the best rates. Thank you."*

If you don't receive money from that bank, it's because another bank or way of financing will be made available to you that will be even better.

When you meet with investors, say:

> *Most Benevolent Outcome*
>
> *"I request a most benevolent outcome for presenting my business plan in such a manner as to be of interest to these investors, and may the outcome be even better than I can hope for or expect. Thank you."*

Their approval and what they offer may pleasantly surprise you. On the other hand, you must be prepared to accept their rejection. It might be for valid reasons, such as they need more information before committing, or your proposal just may not fit their investment portfolio. Whatever the reason, it's because your guardian angel can see farther down the road than you are able to. So be content and keep your hopes up.

For several years, I had been trying to put together a couple of different "packages" of motion pictures. I had co-executive produced several movies but had never taken them from financing all the way through production. During this time, I traveled to Paris, Cannes, Budapest, Prague and Saint Petersburg, Russia, trying to put all the pieces together. I assembled the business plans and budgets, wrote synopses, treatments and even a large part of a script—and yet nothing

became of them. All during that time, I was requesting benevolent outcomes for my efforts. But I was patient, as I know that
benevolent outcomes work perfectly. It just seemed to be taking a long time!

When I had the "inspiration" to do this book, I asked in a
meditation why I had not been successful in putting those film
packages together. The message I received was that doing
those movies would have put me on a completely different
path and I would not have awakened one day inspired to write
this book. I was also told that this book and the books to follow—don't ask; I don't know yet—would be much more
important than any of those films would ever have been. So be
patient. Your guardian angel is working to arrange events in a
way that will be the best for you!

ACCOUNTANTS AND ATTORNEYS

If you have a small business, tax time can be quite stressful.
C.J. in Wisconsin has been requesting benevolent outcomes in
her horse training and healing business for about three years
now, and she periodically sends me emails about her successes. She reported some time ago that she requested a
benevolent outcome when she and her husband visited their
new accountant after previously doing their own tax returns.
The accountant discovered that they had large refunds due for
the past three years, which would more than offset what they
owed in the current year.

Running a small business, you must occasionally utilize
the services of an attorney. Whether it is for contracts with
investors, suppliers, clients or any of the myriad of other
normal needs of a business, a good attorney is important for
the health of your business. When choosing an attorney,
you can state:

> *Most Benevolent Outcome*
>
> *"I request a most benevolent outcome for choosing the right attorney for my business who will charge me correctly for his or her services. Thank you."*

An attorney is sometimes necessary for those times when you cannot settle a dispute. Naturally, I request MBOs for coming to a reasonable solution for any dispute I might have with my clients, so I rarely need the services of an attorney. The last time I needed one to handle a dispute was about four and a half years ago.

I had contracted with a small TV network, and as part of the sales contract they were supposed to do certain things, but they didn't. They were sued, and I was sued along with them, along with another distribution company. When I was served with the papers, I immediately requested a benevolent outcome for myself. Anyone who has been involved in a civil suit knows how many filings of responses must be made. This was a very tight time, as my business had a small cash flow the year after 9/11. I was fortunate to have an old high school friend, who is an attorney in another state, assist me in those responses for several months.

Finally the plaintiff's attorney threatened to go to the judge if I did not hire legal council. Since the legal proceedings were in Houston, I didn't want to hire a Dallas attorney and have to pay for his travel expenses and time, but I didn't know an attorney in Houston. I requested a benevolent outcome for finding an attorney there who could handle my case and charge reasonable rates. The next day when I was putting the trash out in the alley, my neighbor across the way was also out. I knew he was a lawyer, so I asked him if he could recommend one in Houston. He said yes, his nephew was an attorney practicing in Houston!

With my new attorney, we all agreed to mediation in Houston with the plaintiffs, the network and the other distributor. My attorney's boss, who "just happened" to be the top international attorney in Texas, was also present. Naturally I said with a *lot* of feeling:

Most Benevolent Outcome

"I request a most benevolent outcome for myself in this mediation, and may it be even better than I hope or can imagine. Thank you."

The plaintiffs began by demanding five million dollars from the network and one million dollars each from my company and the other distribution company. By the end of the mediation, they had agreed to accept, with everyone paying their own attorney's fees, $400,000 from the network, $100,000 from the other distribution company and *zero* from my company! My only expense was for my attorney, which wasn't cheap, but it was still a whole lot better than it could have been.

If you are an attorney, then you can request MBOs each time you represent your clients in court, mediations and other negotiations. You'll find that your successes will increase, along with the appreciation of your clients.

I trust that by now you can see how requesting benevolent outcomes can make your life less stressful in running your business. It certainly has for me. It's the Gentle Way!

CHAPTER SEVEN

POLITICS

Some of you may think that you have nothing to do with the political process. But any time you have a need to contact someone in your town, city, state, province or national government, you are communicating with a person who possibly was appointed or elected to that position. You should request benevolent outcomes for dealing with these people—certainly if you contribute to their political campaigns. You want them to respond favorably to your request, whether it is to repair a pothole in the street, fix a streetlight that's out or pick up trash—or even for something really big like getting your son or daughter into some institution of higher learning.

RUNNING FOR ELECTION

If you have decided to run for an elected position in your local, state or national government, you can request benevolent outcomes for numerous events. You can request them for meetings with your campaign staff and your supporters, and for debates with the other people running for your position. Since debates can be the catalyst for your election or defeat, you might wish to say:

"I request a most benevolent outcome for my debate, and may it turn out even better than I hoped for or expected. Thank you."

If you are not elected and you had requested a benevolent outcome to be elected, then you have to trust that your guardian angel has something better in store for you. Possibly you need more experience and "seasoning" before you run for office again. Perhaps someone in a higher office will be impressed by you and will offer you a job that will give you better experience or will allow you to run and be elected for an even higher office than the one you originally wanted. Or conceivably you will remain in the private sector and benevolently influence those in office toward what will be the best for their constituents.

GOING BEFORE A CITY COUNCIL

There will be times when you will feel it is necessary to voice your support for or against a proposal before a planning commission or city council. That was the case several years ago when some well-meaning people in my suburb of Dallas decided to buy land near the high school and donate it for a YMCA center for kids. Its location would have been a half block from my house, so it was certainly a concern for us.

They had not considered the fact that the facility they wanted to build would only be used by less than 10 percent of the high school students (according to the student body president), as it was really for younger children. And traffic would have been a mess with parents dropping off and picking up their children just as the high school students were leaving.

Naturally I requested a most benevolent outcome that the building would not be built there, and I appeared before our small-town city council along with a number of my neighbors. We were not against having the center for the children, only that its location should be by the middle school where many more children would use the facilities.

I thought we had lost when the council voted to allow the construction. But then I read that they would only allow the facility to be used by residents of our town. That could not be done, as kids from all over the Dallas area could use any YMCA facility. In the end, the group donated the land to the high school, and tennis courts were built, resulting in a much more gentle use of the land and much less traffic in that area.

FOR A "HIGHER ROAD" OF SERVICE

For those of you elected to an office, you should request a benevolent outcome for choosing the right staff who will work best with you and for you and for the people who elected you. You can also request benevolent outcomes for your meetings with other elected officials and when you meet with your constituents.

If an elected official appoints you to a position, you can request MBOs for working with and for that person, for working with that person's staff and again for working with his or her constituents. All of these requests put you on a "higher road" of service.

ABUSE AND ILLEGAL ACTIVITIES

Let's say that you have been put in a situation that wasn't what you signed up for. Possibly the person you work for is verbally or sexually abusing you, or you have been thrust into corrupt and illegal activities. Then just as I mentioned before for someone in the private sector, you might say:

Most Benevolent Outcome

"I request a most benevolent outcome for revealing this _____ [you can specify here], and may it work out better for me than I can expect or hope for. Thank you."

You can also be more specific here as to whom you are revealing this information to.

In case you haven't noticed (and I'm pretty sure you have), a lot of revelations about illegal activities have recently occurred. Things are just not staying hidden as they did in the past. In my meditations, I have been informed that more than one person in the public sector who reads this book will reveal illegal activities and/or corruption in office. So do you want to be hiding in a closet with the others when someone else opens the door and shines light inside, or do you want to be the one who opens that door? It's your choice.

Serving your town, city, county, province, state or country can be highly rewarding, not so much monetarily, but in knowing you made a difference in helping people lead more benevolent lives—a benevolent outcome for your efforts!

CHAPTER EIGHT

TRAVEL

N ow I would like to give you some ideas on how to utilize benevolent outcomes when you travel, which I sincerely believe will make traveling less stressful for you. I have heard that many people don't travel out of fear. Once you start traveling and meeting people from all over the world, you will find that we are all just different colors of the same cloth. If these stories can encourage more of you to explore our beautiful world, then I'm sure we will have a much more peaceful planet.

FOR ROAD TRIPS

Recently my wife and I flew into Sacramento and drove to Mount Shasta to attend a conference. I naturally requested a benevolent outcome for a safe drive up and, on the return, for the drive back.

On a radio newscast, they said that the California Highway Patrol (CHIP) was getting tough on Interstate 5 and would be ticketing anyone barely over the speed limit. We were driving along on our return and I was passing some slower cars, when an oversize pickup came up behind me. I passed a truck and something told me to let the pickup pass me. After he passed, I then pulled out again to pass another couple of cars. Suddenly a CHIP cruiser burst from behind some trees and bushes on the median divider. I had to zip back into the slower lane to allow him on the road. Off he went and stopped the pickup truck. That could have been me he stopped, but it wasn't—a definite benevolent outcome.

Our two friends, Joy and Bob, recently drove to Las Vegas from Dallas. They requested a most benevolent outcome for their drive, hotel and parking. They told me that each time they passed a police radar speed trap, they were behind trucks and other traffic that had slowed them down. In Las Vegas, they were given exactly the floor of the hotel they wanted and a view of the Strip. And they found the perfect parking space where their car would not be dinged.

WHEN WAITLISTED AT THE AIRPORT

All of you airline employees (and family members of airline employees) know how stressful it can be to stand by on a waitlist for the few seats leftover by no-shows. As I previously mentioned, our daughter was employed with an airline for three and a half years before coming to work for us, during which time we were able to fly free or at a greatly reduced price with a number of airlines. As the family of another airline's employee, we were always at the very bottom of the list, so I would request a most benevolent outcome for getting on that plane.

I can't tell you how many times we were the very last people to board the flight in the last seats. Several times it looked impossible, as there would only be five seats left and I was sixth or seventh on the waitlist. But most of the time there would only be one seat and the two or three people on the waitlist in front of me would pass, waiting for a flight where they could fly together.

FOR SPECIAL DAYS ON VACATION

Requesting MBOs can result in very special days on vacation. Maureen emailed to tell me she requested a benevolent outcome for a dolphin swim she set up for her family in Hawaii. It was the most perfect day anyone could imagine, she said. The water was calm like a lake instead of the usual waves, and the dolphins came twice! The dolphin swim was a special gift for her sister's family, as her sister had been killed in an auto accident a few months before and it was their first Christmas without her.

FOR BUSINESS TRIPS

As an international film and TV program distributor (and before that, as an international tour operator), I must make frequent trips as part of my job. Those trips can be quite stressful. Before the days of requesting benevolent outcomes, I was in two bus wrecks in the mountains, which luckily were minor. I have missed my share of connections. One time coming back from Brazil, we had to turn around five hours into the flight and return to Rio de Janeiro when our plane lost an engine.

As an example of how I utilize requesting benevolent outcomes on business trips, I will begin with a trip to Cannes, France, in April of 2004 for a semiannual TV market. TV stations, networks and DVD companies come from all over the world to buy films and TV shows. On the evening before I departed, I happened to look at my passport while packing and discovered that it had expired the day before!

I immediately requested a most benevolent outcome for making it on the plane the next day. With the help of my daughter and wife, we were able to make a 10:00 A.M. appointment online with the Houston passport office and downloaded the form I needed to fill out to obtain a new passport. I contacted Lufthansa Airline, and they said I could fly from Houston instead of Dallas.

I was on the first Southwest Airlines flight of the day at 6:30 A.M. from Dallas to Houston with all my luggage and took a taxi directly to the passport office. Requesting an MBO for somewhere to leave my luggage, I asked the taxi driver if there was a hotel nearby, and he said yes. We stopped at the hotel and the bellman agreed to store my luggage while I obtained the passport. I was the first person in line when the passport office door opened and discovered that as long as I had an appointment, they would take me when I showed up. Two and a half hours later, I had my passport, picked up my luggage and took a taxi to the airport.

In October I returned to Cannes again. I decided that on this trip I would also exhibit at a small film market in Milan, Italy, which had been moved to four days after the one in Cannes ended. During the week, I was invited by the Milan market organization to take part in a weekend in Lake Como, Italy (George Clooney has a house there that was used in filming *Oceans 12*). They offered complimentary food and tours, but I was supposed to pay for the hotel. I found out that a number of people had also received complimentary hotel accommodations, so I requested an MBO to be given the free hotel too. On the bus, I was right behind the Italian gentleman in charge, and he arranged it so that I was given the hotel accommodations at no cost—in a four-star hotel right on the lakeshore.

During the weekend, a group of us traveled across the Swiss border to a huge manufacturer's outlet, where I bought a couple of Italian suits that required alterations. One of the guys in our car was a Russian, and on the way back, our taxi was held up at the border while the Italians verified his passport and papers. I requested a benevolent outcome, and before long, off we went.

While in Milan, I went downtown to the center of the city to eat at a restaurant recommended by the hotel concierge. It was on a "walking street," where no cars are allowed. At around 11:00 P.M., I headed out to a boulevard to look for a taxi. There were absolutely none that weren't already hired. After several minutes of waiting for an available taxi to pass by, I requested a most benevolent outcome for a taxi to arrive promptly. Before I could complete the request, a taxi zoomed around a corner and I hailed it for the ride back to the hotel.

The day after the Milan market ended, I arose early and took the first train to Lake Como to go across the border to Switzerland to pick up my suits. Lake Como was flooded with people for an international bike race. I headed to the tourist office to ask what bus I could take over the border and was informed that those buses had been cancelled because of the race. About that time, I discovered I had left my passport back in my hotel room in the clothes I had worn the previous evening. The tourist lady saw a look of panic on my face. When I explained my predicament, she suggested I go call the store from a pay phone outside to see what they could do.

Instead, the first thing I did upon leaving the office was to say:

Most Benevolent Outcome

"*I request a benevolent outcome for obtaining my suits. Thank you.*"

I then saw that there was a hotel next door and went in to see if the concierge could assist me. He called the store for me, and they agreed to bring the suits down across the border. He then ordered a taxi but explained that I would have to walk several blocks to the taxi as the streets were closed for the bike race.

But ten minutes later, the taxi arrived—he had been able to work his way through the crowds. After generously tipping the concierge, we headed for the border but were rerouted because of the bike race. I requested another MBO that the person with the suits would wait. Fifty yards from the border checkpoint was a lady patiently waiting for us, suits in hand. I gratefully took them from her, and we headed back to the train station.

The morning I left Milan, I had a very early flight and had to leave the hotel at around 5:00 A.M. I asked the concierge if there was anyone else going at that time who could share a taxi with me for the long ride, but he had no one on his list. I requested a most benevolent outcome for someone to share the taxi, but the next morning I arrived at the front desk with no people in sight. I was resigned to paying for an expensive taxi to the airport when into the lobby walked five or six doctors from the Mayo Clinic who had been in Milan for a cancer conference. They had hired a minibus to take them to the airport and invited me to join them at no charge!

This past April, I had another trip scheduled for the market in Cannes. This time a client of my French buddy, Dominique, offered him his five-bedroom house in Megève, France (a large ski resort), for the week before we went to Cannes. The second day we were there, five of us (Dominique and I, along with two guys from Holland and another from France) drove over to L'Aiguille du Midi, near Mont-Blanc, to ski the famous Vallée Blanche. We had hired a guide, as we were to ski three glaciers (starting from an altitude of 3,800 meters—over 12,000 feet), which had crevices you could fall into. The guide had us put on harnesses so that we could be hauled out of a crevice should we fall into one. Needless to say, I requested a benevolent outcome for the whole day of skiing.

I needed it, as it was late in the ski season and the snow was melting. There had been no snowstorms for over two weeks, making the skiing icy and treacherous. It was especially difficult when we moved from one glacier to the next through the huge chunks of ice. There was little snow left there, and once we even had to take off our skis and just slide down on the glazed ice. Then I fell off a very narrow trail on a steep slope, ending up with one ski laying beneath me. At the bottom of the slope lay a field of blocks of ice, from which I would never have been able to escape. The other skiers had gone over the rise, and only my friend Dominique was behind me. At first I didn't see how I was going to get back up to the trail, as the slope was so steep. It took some work, but eventually with his help I made it back up. If he had not been behind me, I might have been there for an hour or more, waiting until someone made it back up to where I was.

After the TV market, I needed to pick up my ski bag in a far northern suburb of Paris before returning to the States. I took the TGV high-speed train to Paris and spent the night with Neil, a producer-writer friend of mine who was originally from Dallas. I love staying at his apartment, not only for the good conversations, but also because I can watch the Eiffel Tower light show from out of his sixth-floor window before I close my eyes to sleep. That night I requested a benevolent outcome for getting to the airport on time for my flight.

The next morning Neil called for a taxi and heard an automated response saying that one would be on the way. He helped me downstairs with my luggage. This was a Saturday morning, and his apartment is in a residential area with little traffic at that time of day. We waited and waited, but there was no taxi. Neil was about to run to a taxi stand about three blocks away when I spied a taxi far down the street. I requested an MBO that the taxi was headed our way. It turned and went off in another direction, but right behind it was another taxi that proceeded to stop ten feet away from us to drop off a passenger. What a benevolent outcome!

We quickly hired him, and Neil gave him the address. He said he knew the address and off we went. Did he ever! Of all the thousands of taxi drivers in Paris, my driver had grown up only four blocks from where I had to pick up my ski bag. He even pointed out the shop his parents owned before they retired. I'm sure my benevolent angels got a real laugh out of arranging that one! I was also his last passenger of the day, as he had begun work at 3:00 A.M. or so.

BENEVOLENT SYNCHRONICITY

This past June I returned to Budapest for an Eastern European/Central Asian market. I have a Hungarian friend there, Tomas (who goes by Tom internationally), who has expanded from producing to distributing Hungarian movies. He picked me up at the airport and took me to his new office. Like any new company, he has to watch his cash flow as he makes a name for himself internationally. He told me, "Tom you've got to request a benevolent outcome for me to bring in a million euros (about $1,250,000) by the end of the market so that I can expand." Of course, I explained to him that he didn't need me to ask for him, since that is giving away his power to another person.

Our mutual friend Neil from Paris was down to work on funding for a documentary he was going to produce. The second day of the market, a banker, "looking lost," wandered into the booth area where Neil was, and Neil invited him to sit down. The banker explained that he was looking for an Eastern European distributor to invest up to five million euros in but didn't know where to find one. Neil sent him upstairs to Tom's room. Tom told him that he initially needed 200,000 euros and then 1,000,000 euros in six months. The banker asked him to submit a proposal for his bank's consideration the week after the market. Whether Tom receives his funding or not, the point is the synchronicity that put someone on Tom's path who could provide that million euros. Isn't that neat?

REQUESTING A COMPRESSION OF TIME

On my trip from Budapest back to Dallas, the Continental Airlines plane out of Amsterdam was delayed on departure, and it appeared that I had only the slimmest of chances of making my connection in Houston back to Dallas. So naturally I requested a most benevolent outcome that I would make the connection.

In Houston, I was still waiting in the baggage claim area for my luggage with less than twenty minutes to go before my 7:00 P.M. departure. I hadn't even cleared customs, and I knew the flight was two terminals away. Still, I felt that I might make that flight, even though Continental had already given me a boarding pass for a flight two hours later. I kept singing (quietly I might add) the old rock song: "I believe in miracles . . . you sexy thing" ["You Sexy Thing," by Hot Chocolate]. Those were the only words I remembered, so I kept singing them. Some of you might have heard the song reprised recently in a Dr. Pepper commercial.

When I rechecked my bags with Continental, it was three minutes to 7:00 P.M. I asked the agent if I could try to make the flight, and she said sure—but I know she was thinking that there was no chance I would make it. I also requested out loud a compression of time—did you know you can do that too?—and sprinted off. I made it to the gate at 7:10 P.M. I presented my original boarding pass to the gate agent and was the last paying passenger to board. Naturally my bags didn't make the flight, so I requested a benevolent outcome and they were safely delivered later.

At this point I know that if I don't explain compressing time, I will have numerous emails asking about it. This is another one of those things I've experimented with, and I have discovered that it works. Let's say that you have to drive across town to meet some friends. You get a late start and you know you will be late. You say out loud:

Most Benevolent Outcome

"I request a compression in time until I reach my destination and a most benevolent outcome to arrive safely. Thank you."

Then drive normally and *don't look at your watch or car clock!* It doesn't seem to work if you do. When you arrive, you will be amazed at how short a time it took you! Somehow your guardian angel arranges to manipulate time for you.

WHEN MBOs INITIALLY DON'T SEEM TO WORK

There are times when requesting MBOs initially does not seem to work. Last October I returned to Cannes, this time flying through Madrid and connecting to Iberia Airlines. Upon my arrival in Nice, I discovered that none of my three checked bags had made it, even though I had requested a benevolent outcome. The next day, two of the bags were delivered, including my clothes, but the bag with most of my fliers and posters for the booth was still missing. We had to begin the market with minimal poster displays and only two copies of each flier.

I couldn't understand why that bag had not been found, having requested an MBO. On Monday night after the first market day, I did a meditation and asked why I had not received my bag yet. The message I received was that since I had been doing these markets for twenty-three years, I had

become bored, so I set up the baggage delay on a higher con-
sciousness level as a challenge. I was also told that it might be
Wednesday or Thursday before I received the bag.

After the meditation, I requested with a *lot* of feeling that the
bag would arrive the next day. Tuesday afternoon I received a
call that the bag was on its way. It finally arrived at 6:00 P.M.,
at the close of the business day.

On the way back, I flew a regional turboprop on Iberia to
Barcelona for an overnight stay. Two of my bags didn't make it
this time, including the same late bag. Again I did my meditation and asked why. It seems I arranged it so that I wouldn't
have to mess with the extra bags on my way home and they
would be delivered safely in a few days. Six days later, they
arrived. Since they just contained posters, fliers and dirty
clothes, I really had no urgent need for them.

Ask for the Impossible!

I mentioned earlier that you should ask for the impossible,
as the results might exceed anything you could imagine.
During an Alaskan cruise my wife and I took, there were three
ports of call. I had been checking the ten-day forecasts on the
Internet. It had rained every day according to the weather
channel and ship personnel, and the forecast was for more of
the same at each port we were scheduled to dock in. Naturally
my wife and I requested a benevolent outcome for sunny conditions on our first train excursion at Skagway, Alaska. It was
sunny all the way up to the White Horse Pass and back, and
only rained a short time in the afternoon after our return.

When we reached Juneau, Alaska, we had scheduled a whale-
watching tour. We both requested clear weather, since we
would be out on a boat. I found out later that the night before
a whole dinner table of seminar participants I had introduced

MBOs to went around the table, and each one requested a most benevolent outcome for good weather. On our boat tour aboard the new catamaran *Spirit* (what a "wink" at us!), it was slightly overcast with lots of sun breaking through. That afternoon there were even sunnier conditions for the second group of whale watchers.

When we reached Ketchikan, there was not one single cloud in the sky! This is the wettest town in the United States, with an average rainfall of thirteen feet (over four meters) per year. Our local tour guides through the rain forest (who still wore their rain gear) said that normally it was either raining or about to rain. They only have thirteen days of sun per year, so what a most benevolent outcome! This seemed impossible when we requested it.

In this chapter, you have seen a wide variety of occasions when you can request benevolent outcomes to make your trips more enjoyable. There were a couple of exceptions, when the experience was set up on a soul level, but even when traveling the Gentle Way, you want some excitement and challenge in your life! And sometimes the outcome is beyond our understanding of how it was accomplished—the impossible made possible!

CHAPTER NINE

BINGO, CASINOS AND CARD GAMES

Since this book is for all faiths and beliefs, I know there are a number of readers who will not set foot in a casino, including some of my friends and relatives. Those of you who feel that way may choose to skip this chapter. But since there are a large number of people who like to play bingo, go to casinos and play in card games, I will give you some suggestions to make your visits to these establishments more profitable.

A BENEVOLENT OUTCOME FOR BINGO

A few years ago, my family and I took a Caribbean cruise from Houston. On the first day, my daughter and I played bingo, but other activities kept us from playing again until the last day of the cruise. I had requested a most benevolent outcome the first day, but we did not win anything, so I requested a benevolent outcome again on the last day. I said:

Most Benevolent Outcome

"I request a most benevolent outcome for winning at bingo today. Thank you."

My son joined us in the show room along with about three hundred other people. Neither I, nor my son or daughter won anything in the early pots that afternoon.

The "coverall pot" had not been won during the week, and on the last day they play until someone wins it. We were playing multiple cards, and none of us appeared to have any luck, as they kept calling numbers that we did not have. One of my cards was down to about five numbers left, but I expected someone to shout out "BINGO!" any second.

But the next number was one of the five, and the next another, and the next another. And the next one was the next-to-last number. I can assure you, my heart was in my throat. Unbelievably the next number called was my last number, and I shouted out "BINGO!" At the same time, a young man sitting right next to me also yelled "BINGO!"—I'm sure people thought he was my son. I won half of an $8,400 pot along with that young man. What synchronicity! It paid for our cruise. The year before we had taken that same cruise (naturally having requested an MBO for the trip), and a couple of decks had a water leak, which had not affected us, but they offered everyone 50 percent off on their next cruise. Naturally, we took them up on the offer.

AT THE CASINO

I have had mixed luck with casinos until recently. One reason might be because our wholesale tour business took thousands of people to Las Vegas each year. I became acquainted during that time period with the hotel and casino people, and I learned that they knew down to the dollar what the average couple would lose in their casinos during a three-day trip. It truly is a "grind" business. I really did not like losing money that I had worked hard for to these operations, so I limited my casino visits, enjoying the many shows that Las Vegas offered then and continues to offer now.

Recently on an Alaskan cruise with my wife, I decided to wander into the ship's casino. One thing I have learned in my days of running a tour company is that most people subconsciously think they are going to lose when they walk through the casino's doors. I'm sure you've heard or even said such things as: "I'm only taking this much money with me, and when it's gone, I'm stopping," or "I just play to have fun, since I never win." You have to break yourself of this subconscious programming or requesting a benevolent outcome will not work very well, perhaps just limiting you to smaller losses.

One suggestion is to start saying the daily affirmation that appears in Appendix A of this book. You need to say this *every morning* to start reprogramming your subconscious to accept prosperity and abundance.

As I entered the ship's casino each time, I held my arms out with my palms up (although not too obviously) and said:

Most Benevolent Outcome

"*I accept abundance from this casino and request a most benevolent outcome for being a winner today. Thank you.*"

My first time in the casino, I sat down at the blackjack table for about an hour. I was a winner, although not large.

The second time, I came in and sat down. I was up and down, not really getting too far ahead, when the blackjack dealer dealt me the red card from the shoe (which contains several decks of cards that the dealers deal). The red card is the signal to the dealer that it is time to reshuffle all those decks of cards after that game, and the person who receives the card is allowed to cut the decks.

While the dealer finished dealing cards to the other players on the table (I was in the first position), I quietly whispered:

Most Benevolent Outcome

"I request a most benevolent outcome for cutting the cards so that I am a winner during the next round of dealing. Thank you."

I cut the cards, and for the next eight hands or so, I could not lose! Either my hand was better than the dealer's, or for most of the hands, the dealer went over 21 and everyone at the table still in the game won. What fun! It was a happy group of players. I got up and left after that, as I had to dress for a formal dinner.

If you love to play the slot machines, you would say the same thing that I said above upon entering the casino. Perhaps the change girl might suggest a particular machine for you to try, or you might be drawn to a particular one. Be open to these gentle nudgings from your guardian angel.

Although the craps table is not my game, request a benevolent outcome for winning at the table and repeat it again as you are given the dice to throw. I would think it has to work in a way similar to cutting the card decks. There are books on this game—I recently read that there is even a book on how to hold the dice so that they land repeatedly with the same numbers. But it all starts with how you feel about your chances of winning. Welcome abundance from that casino when you walk through the door.

THE LOTTERY

As for the lottery, I've tried it but have never won more than five dollars. Again, perhaps I subconsciously don't think I can win so I don't, or as it was explained to me, some people are meant to win the lottery as a life lesson in how to handle a large amount of money that is suddenly given to them. I think this would be the same life lesson for those who are bequeathed estates and large sums of money. I came to the realization a long time ago that I was going to have to work for my prosperity.

Curly, a friend of mine who works part-time in the drugstore I frequent and who is one of the caretakers for a ninety-eight-year-old elderly lady, plays the lottery all the time, often winning varying amounts. A couple of years ago, she won $20,000, so she has the desire and intention to be successful and sometimes is.

FOR POKER

Poker has recently become an extremely popular game. When you are about to take part in a game, say:

Most Benevolent Outcome

"I request a most benevolent outcome in playing my cards so that I am a winner. Thank you."

You can phrase that as you wish. And you can request an MBO each time you cut the cards during the evening.

Good luck and good fun!

CHAPTER 10

REQUESTING BENEVOLENT OUTCOMES IN DANGEROUS PLACES

I t's amazing how many people live in fear these days. I'm going to show you how to greatly reduce that level of fear through requests for benevolent outcomes when you are in harm's way. If you work in or travel to dangerous places, are in the military, live in a war zone or even work in a dangerous part of an urban city, then requesting benevolent outcomes will protect you, considerably reducing the fear and stress factors.

In a War Zone

Let's say you are in the military, and you find yourself in a war zone. You really don't want to be there, but your duties require you to remain until you rotate back home. Requesting benevolent outcomes will work much better for you if you decide that you would rather not hurt, kill or maim another person, and that you strongly desire not be injured or killed yourself.

So say you are assigned to travel in a convoy from point A to point B. You say out loud:

Most Benevolent Outcome

"I request a most benevolent outcome for our trip to _____. Thank you."

Or if you are on a patrol of some area, say:

> *Most Benevolent Outcome*
>
> "I request a most benevolent outcome for returning from our patrol safely. Thank you."

What may happen in these two examples is that if a roadside bomb is exploded during the trip, it will not be your vehicle that is hit. On the patrol, perhaps your "adversaries" will decide to call it an early night or will be called suddenly to report to another area. It may be a boring patrol, but you will get back to base without any conflict.

Can you imagine what would happen if everyone on both sides of a conflict requested benevolent outcomes to return back to their base safely each day? There could not possibly be a war! I realize this is a dream, but remember, you can ask for the impossible when you request benevolent outcomes! One word of warning: This will absolutely not work if you request an MBO that you kill your adversaries before they kill you. Requesting an MBO for harm to another *doesn't* work. Don't forget that!

If you live in a war zone or dangerous place, you can request benevolent outcomes for even the simplest things, such as going to the grocery store, a restaurant, school or even walking to your car. Say:

> *Most Benevolent Outcome*
>
> "I request a most benevolent outcome for my trip to the store [or to the restaurant or school or work] and back. Thank you."

FOR BURGLARIES

If burglaries and break-ins are a problem in your area, you can say each night, or in the morning before departing for work:

> *Most Benevolent Outcome*
>
> *"I request a most benevolent outcome that my home remains safe and secure from intrusion in any form by others."*

What might happen while you're away is that a policeman might come upon a burglar just before the person breaks into your home, or if a neighbor spies a suspicious person, instead of ignoring that person, he or she might be compelled to call the police.

WORKING IN DANGEROUS PLACES

If you are an aid worker, a government or organization representative, in medical service or any of the myriad of professions that call on you to work or travel in war zones and other dangerous places, it all works the same. Just request a benevolent outcome for moving from one place to the next, for sleeping and eating, or for whatever you feel could put you in danger.

As a reminder, for those of you who work in dangerous places like a convenience store, liquor store, fast food restaurant, construction site or any place that is considered a dangerous job, you can say:

> *Most Benevolent Outcome*
>
> *"I request a most benevolent outcome for my safety at work today. Thank you."*

WHEN SHOPPING

Diane in Michigan emailed me the following story: "I was going to a store one evening, and as is my habit, before I got out of my car, I requested a most benevolent outcome for my errand. I was driving a Hyundai Accent, which is not an expensive car, but it was almost brand-new at that time and looked very good. I had parked in a small lot in back of the store. After I exited my car, I noticed a young man standing in the lot a few spaces down. As I passed him, he made a remark to me about my "nice car." Without even thinking about it or breaking my stride, I thanked him sincerely and added in a friendly manner that it was very economical too, and then I entered the store.

"While in the store, I suddenly started shaking, and it occurred to me that the young man had robbery, at the least, in mind. But I calmed down almost immediately, since I realized that I was in the store and safe. I knew that if he was still there when I was ready to leave, I could ask an employee to escort me to my car. However, I had a strong intuition that he would not be there. I added a request for a most benevolent outcome to getting safely home and was not surprised to see that the young man was nowhere in evidence when I left. I thanked God and the angels most sincerely!"

Diane mentioned that she had been requesting benevolent outcomes for quite some time now and that her "life has flowed smoothly, benevolently and miraculously as a result." I couldn't say it any better.

DANGEROUS PROFESSIONS

Two of the most dangerous professions these days are being a police officer and being a firefighter. These professions are constantly featured in TV news broadcasts due to the danger of these types of work. These people never know when the next call could put their lives in mortal danger. If you are a police officer or a firefighter, say each day:

Most Benevolent Outcome

"I request a most benevolent outcome for returning from my shift safely today. Thank you."

This request each day for a benevolent outcome to return back to the station safely will set in motion circumstances that will allow that benevolent outcome to occur.

Another dangerous profession is that of a prison guard. These guards must work in a very negative environment each day, with inmates who are dejected and angry that they are incarcerated. Requesting a benevolent outcome for safety during your shift each day will make this job much easier and less stressful.

For Those in Prison

Let's not forget the inmates themselves. They are kept in sometimes barbaric conditions that offer them no hope of redemption. There is little or no training to prepare them for their release so that they can make an honest living and become law-abiding citizens. In prison, there may be gangs to contend with or other prisoners who can take offense at the slightest perceived insult.

If you are incarcerated, you can request benevolent outcomes each time you go for food, to the shower, to exercise in "the yard," to the common area near your cell or on work detail. If you are imprisoned unjustly, then request an MBO for assistance in your sentence being overturned. Ask for what seems impossible!

Illegal Immigrants

This next section is for those who live outside the United States, Europe and the major Asian nations. If you are an illegal immigrant about to make your way across a border in the hopes of feeding your family, you run the risk of arms and legs being severed under the wheels of trains, of bandits who prey on people in your situation, of smugglers who might take your money and leave you to die in hostile environments, of drowning in rivers or oceans, or of being captured by border patrols and sent back home to poverty.

At the start of your travel, you can say:

> *Most Benevolent Outcome*
>
> *"I request a most benevolent outcome for my trip to _____. Thank you."*

Each day you can request an MBO for riding the train in safety, for crossing rivers or oceans, for traveling safely through areas with gangs of bandits, for dealing with smugglers and for making it across the border safely to your destination.

After you reach your destination, you can first request a benevolent outcome for finding a good job. Then each day you can request an MBO that you be safe and free from deportation and able to stay as long as necessary in that country.

PROSTITUTION

One dangerous profession that no one likes to talk about is prostitution. These men and women, boys and girls, are in danger every day of their lives. Their families have sold many of them into sexual slavery, or they have run away from physical and sexual abuse. They have been corrupted and duped by pimps, and have suffered more sexual and physical abuse.

For those of you in this profession, say:

> *Most Benevolent Outcome*
>
> *"I request a most benevolent outcome to return home safely and disease free today. Thank you."*

You can also say:

> *Most Benevolent Outcome*
>
> "*I request a most benevolent outcome for finding a way out of prostitution and obtaining whatever I need to succeed in life. Thank you.*"

Remember to ask for the impossible—you just might receive it!

For the Work Commute

Many people would not think that commuting to work in a large urban city is dangerous, but tell that to commuters who read about or have seen road rage, multicar pileups and carnage on the road. Several years ago, I was headed for Cannes, France, to another TV market, and I rented a car at the Nice Airport for the twenty-minute drive on the six-lane toll road between the two towns. I requested an MBO for the drive. Ten minutes later I was glad I did, as a small car passed by me going too fast. It lost control about three hundred meters up the road, hit the median barrier and bounced back onto the highway, coming to rest sideways across two lanes of traffic. Had I reached the scene five seconds sooner, I would have been in the middle of his wreck. I slowed down to about 16 kph (10 mph) and went past the car using the far right-hand lane.

For you commuters who take trains, subways or buses to work, I'm sure you've paid close attention to the news about the bombings of the subways and buses in such cities as Madrid and London. As you head for the station each morning and afternoon, say:

> *Most Benevolent Outcome*
>
> "*I request a most benevolent outcome for arriving safely at my work [or home]. Thank you.*"

This takes the fear factor down to a minimum level, as you know that if there is a major problem, you will not be involved.

PICKPOCKETS

In many major cities of the world, pickpockets are a problem. Years ago when I used to exhibit at the Cannes Film Festival, a journalist friend of mine lost his wallet to a pickpocket while passing through a crowd on the street. It was a known fact that the pickpockets would come down to Cannes because many of the people attending carried a lot of money.

Just recently I spent a night in downtown Barcelona. The first thing the front desk people warned me about was to watch my wallet when I went out for dinner, as pickpockets were working in the area. So request a benevolent outcome for your safety and the safety of all of your personal effects during your walk or excursion in a city.

DANGERS AT SCHOOL:
GANGS, VIOLENCE AND INJURY

Attending school these days can be dangerous both for the students and for the teachers and principals. There have been numerous beatings and shootings in schools resulting in death and injury to the students and adults. Gangs at some schools can cause the students and teachers much stress and fear. Plus, there are parents who are going through difficult divorces who try to take their children out of school when they are not allowed to see them under court order.

Injuries can also occur during school in sports, science classes, cheerleading and other school-sponsored activities. If you are a student or teacher, say:

> *Most Benevolent Outcome*
>
> *"I request a most benevolent outcome for my safety going to and from school, and during the time I am at school and involved in all school activities. Thank you."*

RISKY SPORTS

Speaking of sports, there are a number of sports that have some risk attached—some much more than others. Take sky-diving, for example. Many years ago when I was in the Army and stationed in Korea with the "peacekeeping" force, I used to take flying lessons at a small airport on a sandbar in the middle of the Han River. One day we saw some skydivers jump out of a plane. One of the men had a chute that only partially opened. He worked with it until finally he opened his reserve chute. He was a big guy and the chute did not slow him down completely, and he was carted off the field with a hip injury. I never wanted to try skydiving after that. But of course, now I could say:

> *Most Benevolent Outcome*
>
> *"I request a most benevolent outcome for all of my jumps today to be safe and trouble free. Thank you."*

As I mentioned earlier, skiing is another sport that I know a lot about. I learned to ski in college and used that knowledge to start my first business—a singles ski club that would take single adults to Colorado, New Mexico and Utah. I had only a couple of injuries over the years, with the worst being a shattered shoulder, which happened at Aspen, Colorado, on the first day of the ski season. I was the first injury of the year and was supposed to be taking care of three hundred people on the trip! We did have some close calls on our bus trips to the mountains, including two potentially bad fender-benders caused by drunk drivers on the road. So request a benevolent outcome for the drive to and from the ski area, and then say each time you ski:

> *Most Benevolent Outcome*
>
> *"I request that my skiing [or snowboarding] today be safe and enjoyable. Thank you."*

Scuba (or underwater) diving is a wonderful sport, taking you into another world of beautiful plants, reefs and more varieties of fish than you could ever imagine. During my tour wholesaler days, we ran trips to the Cayman Islands in the British West Indies four days a week. I'm sure you've read reports of people getting the bends (decompression sickness) from coming up too fast or even dying in underwater caves or wrecks. The brother of my agent in Grand Cayman tried to set a world record for a one-tank dive and never came back, so it can be dangerous. I suggest that each day you state:

> *Most Benevolent Outcome*
>
> *"I request a most benevolent outcome for my safety today during my dives. Thank you."*

You can request benevolent outcomes for safety during all your sports outings—football, volleyball, baseball, track and field, swimming and so on. Request benevolent outcomes for each time you practice and for each of your games.

IDENTITY THEFT AND COMPUTER VIRUSES

Here is a danger that seems to have everyone fearful these days: identity theft. Say out loud:

> *Most Benevolent Outcome*
>
> *"I request a most benevolent outcome that my personal established identity in all of its forms be safe and secure from harm and from corruption by others. Thank you."*

How about that for taking your power back?

Worried about computer viruses? You can request protection for your computer with the following:

> *Most Benevolent Outcome*
>
> *"I request a most benevolent outcome that my computer hard drive and all my programs remain safe and secure from harm and corruption by others. Thank you."*

You can bring safety into your life when you request benevolent outcomes for traveling, working and living. It is the Gentle Way.

CHAPTER ELEVEN
THE RADIANT EFFECT

W hen you request a benevolent outcome, you are requesting something specific for yourself. Your friends and family have to request their own benevolent outcomes. But I did begin noticing that when I requested a benevolent outcome, it also had a benevolent effect on the people surrounding me at the time of the request.

OTHERS BENEFIT FROM YOUR MBO REQUESTS

Let's look closely at what happens when you request MBOs. Take, for example, the request for a close parking place. If you have your friends or family with you, they benefit from you finding a well-located parking space. It could be raining, snowing or a hot day, or you or another person in your car might have a physical problem that would make a long walk difficult. They all benefit from your request for a benevolent outcome.

When you drive to and from work and request a benevolent outcome for safely arriving, all those cars around you come under the influence of your MBO request. And when you are on that subway, train or bus to and from work, there is a radiant effect from your request for a benevolent outcome for safely arriving, as the other people in that vehicle will probably arrive safely too.

When you applied for that job, the company that hired you and your coworkers all benefited, creating the radiant effect. The company benefited by being coupled with you, since this was a benevolent outcome, and your new coworkers benefited by getting someone who is the best for that position and probably the most enjoyable person to work with.

When our friends in the high-end painting and contracting business requested a benevolent outcome for landing a new client, the people who hired them benefited from their expertise and attention to detail. Their workers benefited by having additional work to keep them busy for several months.

Each time I request an MBO in my business when I am negotiating with a new client, I know that it will also be in his or her best interest to buy from my company. We're good and honest people to work with and have gained a reputation over many years as a trustworthy supplier. My request for a benevolent outcome affects them in a positive Gentle Way.

In an earlier chapter, I mentioned the trip my son, his friend, his friend's father and I took to Yellowstone and how I had requested a benevolent outcome for being "bumped" on our return flight. We were not bumped, but we were all given first-class seats for volunteering. My MBO request had the great radiant effect of all of us traveling in first class together. It was a great treat, not only for them, but also for me in experiencing their enjoyment and happiness.

MBOs Affect the Safety of Others

If you have to act as a whistleblower to report sexual abuse or misconduct or to report illegal activities where you work, you naturally will request a most benevolent outcome for yourself in reporting these actions. Your angels will take care of you, but the radiant effect can extend far beyond that. There may be other people suffering as you are, and they will no longer have to bear the pain. They may even have the courage to add their voices. If this involves illegal business acts, then you may save hundreds or even thousands of jobs by getting rid of the "bad apples." Possibly thousands of people who own shares in your company will not lose the money they invested.

If you're in the military and in a war zone, when you requested that benevolent outcome for arriving safely at your destination, at the very least the other people in your vehicle will arrive safely too. But also perhaps all the other vehicles in the convoy will arrive safely because the bomb that was supposed to go off didn't for some reason, thereby saving their lives and those of any civilians who might have been in the blast zone.

When you are on patrol and request a benevolent outcome to return safely from your mission, the patrol will probably return with no encounters. You're safe, but so are all of your buddies who were on the patrol with you. Again, it's the radiant effect. And I should take this one step further and mention that all the people you do encounter and do not encounter also return home safely too, be they civilians or soldiers!

As a civilian living in a war zone, when you request that benevolent outcome for going to work, to school or even to the grocery store, it has a radiant effect on all those who come in contact with you wherever you walk or drive. It may well be your family and friends, but it might also be strangers on the street, at the market where you shop, in the restaurant where you eat or at the nightclub you attend.

If you are incarcerated in prison or are a prison guard, requesting a benevolent outcome each day for your safety again affects all those around you. As you move about during the day, that radiant effect follows you around.

It's the same for policemen, firemen and paramedics. Everyone who works with them receives the benefit of their MBO requests for safety. Plus, the public they serve benefits too. When they respond to a call, there is always the chance of an accident happening on the way. If there's no accident, there are no injuries for themselves, their coworkers and for whoever might have been involved in the vehicle crash.

In a recent chapter, I told the story of the guy in the pickup who was stopped and ticketed for speeding by the California Highway Patrol during a drive from Mount Shasta back to Sacramento. That probably was a radiant effect both for him, in that he'll slow down, and also for the other drivers he might have endangered. I know that to be a fact—since my son was stopped for speeding, he drives much more responsibly now!

MBOs Lead to a More Gentle Life for Everyone!

When I was in the casino on the Alaskan cruise and cut the card decks after requesting a benevolent outcome, I won a number of games, but so did the rest of the people sitting at my blackjack table. I had a great feeling sitting there knowing that I was a catalyst for their good luck and good cheer!

Even when you ask for a benevolent outcome for a taxi, there is a radiant effect. Possibly that taxi driver has not had a fare in a few minutes and needs the business. Something tells him to turn down the street you're waiting on, and he picks up a nice fare, and a safe one too. Both of you benefit from your request.

When a number of us requested sunny skies at the ports in Alaska, hundreds if not thousands of people were affected by our request. All of the tours could be operated, including those with helicopters and airplanes. It was positive income for the tour operators and their staffs. All of the cruise passengers enjoyed the rain-free days, and I'm sure the shops along the docks did exceptional business while we were in port.

You can look back at the chapters you've read so far and see numerous instances where someone else was affected in a positive way by those requests for benevolent outcomes. It will be the same for you too. You just have to make requesting MBOs a habit, and your life and the lives of those around you will be much more gentle!

CHAPTER TWELVE

LIVING PRAYERS

L iving prayers and benevolent outcomes are similar, like "kissing cousins," but they are different. Whereas a benevolent outcome is something you request for yourself, a living prayer is something you can say when you feel the need to ask for benevolent assistance *for someone else.* That person or those persons may not know how to request it for themselves, or they may be in such great danger that they are unable to say anything at all.

HURRICANES AND OTHER DEVASTATING STORMS

Here in the United States we had a terribly destructive hurricane in 2005 named Katrina. I was touched by the news stories that showed people wading in waist-deep water and being plucked off rooftops by helicopters. I was not physically able to assist them, so I said:

Living Prayer

"I ask that all those beings who are in danger and need help receive all the assistance they need from any and all beings who can help them."

Let's take, for example, a disaster that might happen on the other side of the world from you. It might be an earthquake or a hurricane. These events happen all the time. It's been reported in the news that hurricanes are increasing in strength due to global warming. You know from news reports that when these storms occur, people are often injured and in danger of dying, or are left without food, water and shelter. In the event of any large-scale disaster, you can say:

Living Prayer

"I ask that all of the beings in _____ [say the specific or even general location] who are in misery and need assistance receive all the help, support and love that they need from all those beings who can help them."

As you can see, you can change the wording to fit the circumstances. You don't have to use my exact wording.

You can state the actual location, or if you are not sure, just name the country. The reason you say "beings" is that those in danger might be people, their pets or animals of all different kinds. In the aftermath of Katrina, on TV you could see dogs up on rooftops either with or without their owners. Many pets were rescued by goodhearted people who went out in boats to find them. Using the word "beings" for those who can help could include men, women, children, dogs, animals or angelic beings. You don't want to put limits on your request.

LIVING PRAYER IN ACTION

I first read about living prayers in the previously mentioned book *Council of Creators* by Robert Shapiro. He later expanded upon this concept in other writings, but for awhile I couldn't see the difference between "ask" and "request," so I stayed with requesting benevolent outcomes. But it's quite simple in concept.

In living prayer statements, you say, "I ask." In my meditations I mentioned that I couldn't see much difference between the words "request" and "ask." I was told to go and look them up in a dictionary. Somewhat chastened, I did. To summarize very long definitions, "request" is used to ask for a specific action, whereas "ask" is a more general request. They are similar words but are not exactly the same.

Living prayers contain simple words, but they are *powerful*. By asking you will feel better. You will not have feelings of helplessness or frustration. Living prayers are *things*. Angelic beings act *instantaneously* and there is an *energy* that is created by your request and their actions. It has been described to me that if you could see these prayers, they have the appearance of colorful streamers of love and feelings as they arrive from all over the world to the location of a disaster, sometimes in the millions.

Normally, you will never know if your living prayer actually assisted someone—you just have to have faith that it did. But there are occasions when you do know. Recently, when my wife and I boarded an airplane for a flight from San Diego back to Dallas, a couple sat down in the row just in front of us. Shortly thereafter there was that look of panic on their faces which I described earlier when I discovered I didn't have my passport in Lake Como, Italy. I whispered where only my wife could hear:

Living Prayer

"I ask that any and all beings assist this couple with their problem."

We couldn't hear all of what they were saying, except something about the gate area or car, but the woman got up and left the plane.

About ten minutes later, she came back with a look of relief, carrying her purse. She had left it at the security checkpoint and "fortunately" no one had picked it up except a security person, who held the purse until she reclaimed it. Both were happy and kissed each other before settling back to enjoy the flight. My wife and I had been able to see a living prayer in action.

FOR INCIDENTS ON THE NEWS

As with requests for benevolent outcomes, you must say a living prayer for what you want, not what you don't want. Let's use apartment fires as an example. People live in close quarters in urban areas, and regrettably, fires result from people smoking in bed, old electrical wiring and many other reasons. Television stations broadcast these events live if they happen during the news broadcast. There you are, sitting in your living room or even at the dinner table, and you see or hear that people and possibly their pets are trapped.

Don't say, "Don't let that building collapse or let the fire burn those beings." Rather say:

Living Prayer

"I ask that those beings inside that apartment building remain safe until rescued, that the firemen perform their duties safely and that the apartment building remains stable and strong until everyone is safe."

You can even shorten this request and say:

Living Prayer

"I ask that those beings inside that apartment building remain safe until rescued."

Change the words to fit the circumstances.

Recently on one of those newscasts, there was a story about a female journalist who had been captured by terrorists who threatened to kill her if their demands were not met. Upon hearing that, I said:

Living Prayer

"I ask that this woman journalist be given all the assistance and comfort possible immediately from any and all beings."

You may not be able to do anything individually, but can you imagine the effect of thousands of these requests being acted on instantly by angelic beings?

FOR LOVED ONES IN DANGEROUS PLACES

For those of you with a family member in a dangerous place, you can say:

Living Prayer

"I ask that my loved one _____ [say his or her name] be completely safe in _____ and return home."

You may wish to say this each day, but try to say it differently. Perhaps you name the camp location one day, the city or town the next, the province your loved one is in another day, the area of the country the next and the name of the country the following day. Then if he or she comes home on leave or at the end of his or her tour of duty, you would say:

Living Prayer

"I ask that _____'s trip home be safe and benevolent."

INCLUDING YOURSELF IN LIVING PRAYERS

After requesting benevolent outcomes for years, living prayers are a more recent development for me (although not as recent as

"I hope" requests, which are covered in the next chapter). Below you will see examples of times when you will say a living prayer for both yourself *and* your loved ones. In the earlier chapters, I did not want to separate the benevolent outcomes that would be for you and your family from benevolent outcomes for yourself. In my experience, there seems to be only a small difference if you are asking for a benevolent outcome that includes you and a living prayer for yourself and, say, your family. I believe this is because of the radiant effect. Just be sure to say a living prayer if it is for someone else.

With that in mind, you can say living prayers for others and you can include yourself. As an example, say you're in a dangerous war zone, as I mentioned before, and your group must move from one place to another. You might say:

Living Prayer

"I ask that myself and others remain completely safe as we travel to _____."

On patrol you might state:

Living Prayer

"I ask that myself and others remain completely safe during our patrol and return safely to our base."

Say you live in an area threatened by severe storms, such as tornadoes or hurricanes like Katrina. In this case, you would say:

Living Prayer

"I ask that I and my family be completely safe in this storm and that my town remains safe as well."

Change the words to fit the circumstances. If you and your loved ones are trapped in a damaged or collapsed house, or by floodwaters, you could say:

> *Living Prayer*
>
> "I ask that I and my loved ones remain safe and that we receive help immediately from any and all beings."

We all see and read stories about physical and sexual abuse in our communities. But there are those reading this book who are actually experiencing abuse on a daily basis. If you live in a household where there is physical or sexual abuse, you definitely should say:

> *Living Prayer*
>
> "I ask that my safety and that the safety of my children be guaranteed now and in the future in a way that is benevolent for us all."

If the reason for the abuse is because of an addiction to alcohol or drugs, you can say:

> *Most Benevolent Outcome*
>
> "I ask that any and all beings come to the aid of _____ and assist him or her in the most benevolent way possible for our family."

Remember, you can ask for what seems impossible!

KEEP LIVING PRAYERS SIMPLE AND PURE

Keeping in mind that this book is for people of all religious faiths and beliefs, some of you will ask if you can include the name of your religious deity when you say these living prayers. Certainly you can if you wish, but I have been told in my meditations that the living prayers work best if kept simple and pure. As I mentioned above, the angelic beings who handle these know *instantly* that you have said a living prayer and will act upon it. Nothing additional need be said.

IN FINDING A MATE AND SETTLING DOWN

When you are looking for someone to spend your life with, you should request a living prayer, as you are involving someone else. Say:

Living Prayer

"I am asking that I will soon encounter the most wonderful person for me, that he or she likes and loves me just the way I am, and that I like and love him or her just the way he or she is—that we can grow together, resulting in the most benevolent outcome for me."

After you find that perfect person, you typically have to find somewhere to live together. This living prayer can also be used if you must relocate to another town, city or country:

Living Prayer

"I ask that the perfect home in the best location for myself and my family be made available and known to us right now, and that we can live in it as long as we need in the most benevolent way possible."

When you have meetings with the teachers or counselors at your children's school, you might state:

Living Prayer

"I ask that this meeting result in the most benevolent outcome for my child's education and future."

Concerning Your Relationship with Others

Business relationships can be pleasant or quite tumultuous. I had one of the latter many years before I learned about benevolent outcomes. All of these are learning experiences, but remember, we are taking the Gentle Way. So you can state:

Living Prayer

"I ask that the perfect business partner (or partners) make themselves known to me now and that this results in the most benevolent outcome for me."

Again, this involves other people, so it can be said as a living prayer, even though you are requesting that it be a benevolent outcome for you.

There are times when all of us make mistakes that either inadvertently or sometimes intentionally cause others stress and problems. When that happens, say the following *with feeling and sincerity:*

Living Prayer

"I ask that any consequences or effects that may be harmful to others on the basis of my recent actions be calmed, healed, cared for and set right."

Saying this in your own words is best.

Concerning Disease

Every year we seem to hear about some new disease that threatens the health of people in some part of the world. Recently it's been the bird flu, and before that it was mad cow disease. Next year it will probably be something else. Each year your newspapers, magazines and radio and TV news programs report the disease's spread and the number of deaths attributed to it. You're concerned, but what can you do about it except worry? I suggest you say:

Living Prayer

> "I ask that all those beings in _____ who are suffering from the _____ disease immediately receive all the assistance they need from all those beings who can help them."

FOR ARTISTIC COLLABORATION

If you are a writer, you want to write the best story, article or book that you possibly can to be the most successful you can be. When I started writing this book, I said:

Living Prayer

> "I ask that all those beings who can collaborate with me assist me now in writing the best book in the most benevolent way for me, and that this result in an excellent book that I can present successfully to my publisher."

Change the words to fit your writing circumstances.

If you are a filmmaker, you can say something similar to the above. As an example, you may wish to say:

Living Prayer

> "I ask that all those beings who can collaborate with me assist me now in creating the best film that will appeal to the widest audience, and that this result in the most benevolent outcome for me."

You will find that in saying this, it will attract to you the best writers, directors, cameramen, actors and crew people— whomever you need to be as successful as you can be.

FOR THE GLOBAL COMMUNITY AND BENEVOLENT POLITICAL DECISIONS

In case you haven't noticed, one result of the exploding world population is that more and more we will have to learn how to get along with people of different races, cultures and beliefs. Possibly you and those in the area or country you live in have felt uncomfortable living and working with people who seem so different than you. What can you do? Start by saying:

Living Prayer

"I ask that I and all my friends, family and neighbors live and work together in a most benevolent way with all other human beings now and in the months and years to follow."

This living prayer and thousands like it will make the integration into a world community much less stressful and fearful.

Politics is always a subject on which everyone has an opinion. Even in a completely free society, governments can't make public all the reasons for the policies and decisions they make, even if they are in your best interest. But those same government leaders are human and can make mistakes or can be influenced by people and companies that do not have your best interests at heart. So I suggest that you say:

Living Prayer

"I ask that my government leaders act benevolently and with compassion, and carry out policies that will be the most benevolent for my country and the world."

On another day you can change this and simply say:

> *Living Prayer*
>
> *"I ask that my leader, _____ [say his or her name], be moved to make the most benevolent decisions and policies that will serve the needs of all our people and will be the most benevolent for the world community."*

This must be said in a sincere way, as it will not work if you are disparaging or joking in your tone of voice. I know that's hard sometimes when you constantly see and hear the leaders of your country as the butt of jokes on TV, radio and in the press. But do be serious and sincere.

If your country borders on another country or is surrounded by countries, the decisions of the leaders of those countries can affect your life and your family's lives. The Middle East is a good example of this, with many families' lives shattered by the decisions of a few. For the leader or leaders of another government, say:

> *Living Prayer*
>
> *"I ask that the leaders of _____ [say the name of the country] make decisions and carry out the most benevolent policies that will serve the needs of their country and affect our country in the most benevolent way."*

FOR WORLD PEACE AND MOTHER EARTH

I really started learning about living prayers when I decided to ask for a benevolent outcome for world peace. It was explained to me in my meditations that different angelic beings handle these general requests. It was suggested that I say:

> *Living Prayer*
>
> *"I ask that the general attitudes of all peoples on the Earth become compatible with the general attitudes of all other people on Earth."*

This is a good one to say right now. On another day, you can say:

> *Living Prayer*
>
> *"I am asking that the hearts of all beings come to love peace, cherish it and involve themselves in its creation."*

Say these requests only *one time*. That's all that's needed.

Perhaps you are concerned about the environment. Maybe you think that a national park, forest or refuge is not receiving all the assistance it should from your government. Then say:

> *Living Prayer*
>
> *"I ask that all the beings who live and visit _____ be supported and cared for through the actions of my government's leaders in the most benevolent way they are able."*

For all of nature and the environment, you can state:

> *Living Prayer*
>
> *"I ask that Mother Earth replenish herself in a most benevolent way, with support from all beings to replenish all portions of herself that humans on Earth have removed or changed.*

Another environmental request is:

Living Prayer

"I ask that all industries that are harming beings and Mother Earth be encouraged and discover benefits to utilizing other resources to produce their desired results in a more benevolent way for all beings, including Mother Earth."

You can make this request more specific, naming the industry or company.

For the many of you who don't believe that our planet is the only inhabited one in trillions and trillions of planets, you might state:

Living Prayer

"I ask that we be contacted by only those loving, benevolent beings who will assist us in a most benevolent way for our whole planet and all beings living here, for now and into the far future."

This last living prayer might be answered sooner than you think!

LIVING PRAYER REVIEW

* Living prayers and benevolent outcomes are similar; however, one "asks" whereas the other "requests."
* Living prayers are to be said for other people, although you can include yourself.
* Living prayers are to be said as simply as possible.
* Living prayers are acted upon instantaneously by angelic beings.
* Living prayers are powerful energies.
* Living prayers make a difference.

CHAPTER THIRTEEN

"I HOPE" REQUESTS

I recently discovered using hope as a benevolent request on a visit to our friends, Don and Karen, who now live in San Diego. (I spoke earlier in the book about how Karen found some important papers by requesting a benevolent outcome.)

MY DISCOVERY OF "I HOPE" REQUESTS

My wife and I had not been to San Diego for a number of years, so the four of us did touristy things: taking in the large wildlife preserve and going to the Scripps Oceanic Institute's amazing aquarium. For lunch one day, we were in the quaint town of Escondido. We drove slowly down the main street looking for a restaurant. The town has parallel parking on the street, and most of the spaces were filled. Suddenly a car pulled out just in front of us, and I knew that this was where we were supposed to stop and park (sometimes it seems my guardian angel is so used to my requests for MBOs that they are provided with a "wink" at me). In front of us was a small French bakery that also served a lunch menu.

It was a warm, pleasant sunny day, so we decided to eat outside in a small fenced area in front. We were enjoying our lunch and conversation until a man came out of the store-front next-door with a wheelbarrow. He and two young boys were obviously remodeling inside, and he had decided to clean cement from his wheelbarrow. He began to loudly scrape the insides with a shovel. Not only was this noisy, but also dusty. There were two parties of people even closer to him than we were, so everyone was annoyed. This went on for several minutes.

Finally I said with some feeling:

I Hope
> "I hope that he's through now!"

He immediately stopped scraping the wheelbarrow, put the shovel down and took the wheelbarrow back inside. I was quite surprised, and my friend Don started laughing, having also seen what happened. I knew that the man couldn't have heard me, but it was still embarrassing, as I felt like I had somehow commanded the man to stop. We finished our lunch without further interruptions.

The next morning I meditated about this, and the message I received was that the request "I hope" is another form of a benevolent request for something to happen that involves someone else. The other person does not have to comply if he or she does not wish to, so it is purely benevolent. "Hope" is defined in *Webster's Dictionary* as "desire accompanied with expectation of obtaining what is desired or belief that it is obtainable." In this instance, it was explained that the man was close to finishing. When I said that I hoped he was finished, he complied and stopped cleaning further.

WAYS TO USE HOPE REQUESTS

So far, I have not tried to utilize "I hope" requests very often. One might use it in a circumstance where you are in a busy restaurant and you say:

> *I Hope*
> **"I hope that our server comes to take our order now."**

I tried this recently at a restaurant where I could see our server mixing two drinks for someone. He didn't come, but another server walked by, asked us if we needed anything and took care of our request.

Or possibly it could be said when you are in a busy store and wish that the salespeople would give you assistance immediately. If they don't, it's because they truly are busy and can't directly respond. If you need a paper or project approved, you could also say:

> *I Hope*
> **"I hope that this meets with approval."**

If you wish someone to call for either business or personal reasons, you could state:

> *I Hope*
> **"I hope that _____ calls me today."**

You may wish to follow that up with a request for a benevolent outcome for the results of that call.

I look upon "I hope" requests as supplementing your benevolent outcome requests and living prayers. I'll be interested to hear how you have been able to utilize these hope requests.

CHAPTER FOURTEEN

FINAL THOUGHTS

I n this book, I have presented you with a more gentle way of living. I have given you a way to be constantly in touch with your guardian angel and guides.

If you do not make requesting benevolent outcomes and asking for living prayers a habit, it will be like the old rock song says, "We are but a moment's sunlight, fading in the grass" ["Let's Get Together," The Youngbloods]. Your memories of requesting and recieving benevolent outcomes will fade away, and you will be back to reacting to life instead of acting to make it the best, most peaceful, most fun, least stressful and least fearful life for your circumstances.

Making a habit of requesting benevolent outcomes has been the most difficult thing for my friends to do. Don't think that you should just request benevolent outcomes for the "important things," as if you are a person given only three wishes. You can request MBOs thousands of times. I mentioned before that I have requested benevolent outcomes somewhere between ten and fifteen thousand times, and I haven't run out of those "forms" yet.

I must also reemphasize that the more you request benevolent outcomes, the more you will be tuned in to recognizing the messages and changes of circumstances that are sent by your guardian angel. I now notice even with simple requests of an MBO for my drive across the city how spaces in traffic open up for me, how the traffic policeman has just pulled over someone else a few seconds before I arrive and how dangerous drivers pass by giving me a wide berth. I'm now much more aware of my surroundings, and you will be too.

That's why I have suggested that you place reminders around your home or office, small signs that constantly remind you of this until you don't have to be reminded anymore. I have suggested that you make several signs. Just make a sign by hand with your kid's crayons or with a large colorful felt-tip pen—anything that will catch your eye each day and evening. If you haven't done so, stop and do so now!

If you have already been requesting benevolent outcomes, I'm sure you have been seeing successes already for the smaller mundane happenings. If you started out requesting MBOs for only the big, important events, then you may not have received resolution yet. Don't believe that nothing is happening. Rome wasn't built in a day! Be patient—as I'm repeatedly told in my meditations—and request the small events.

In the following pages, you will find "bonus points," also commonly known as appendixes. These are extra suggestions that, during the time you are requesting benevolent outcomes and living prayers, will improve your life even more.

I will remind you again: I did not invent talking to angels. This has been going on for thousands of years. I just tried out some concepts, and they worked for me, so I'm passing them along to you. You've read many of the mistakes I've made over the years in this book—with MBOs saving me—and I can assure you that there are many more to come. That's part of the adventure of life. Think of me as a friend, and if you ever meet me, give me a hug. That's all I ask or want. Hugs are great!

So I'll see you in my next book, if not before. Now I will wish you something that you can say to all those people you meet and to dogs, cats, animals, trees, flowers, lakes, houses and anything else you encounter on this beautiful planet of ours: Good life!

BONUS POINTS:

AN EXPLANATION OF
THE FOLLOWING APPENDIXES

This is not your normal appendix section. The following pages will give you extra work and methods that are beyond the basic scope of this book. In college, my son was given extra work that he and the other students could do to earn bonus points in the courses they were taking. That's why I named it "Bonus Points."

Look at the following pages that way. You don't have to try them out or experiment with them to be successful in requesting benevolent outcomes. But they will enrich your life as a bonus should you decide to incorporate any of them into your daily life.

If you do have a great success story, please email me. I will probably write a sequel to this book. In it I will relate stories from around the world to encourage more people to adapt MBO requests into their daily lives. Please contribute and send your stories to: stories@thegentlewaybook.com. Good life!

—Tom T. Moore

AN MBO REMINDER FOR YOUR MIRROR

In order to assist you in remembering to request benevolent outcomes each day so that this can become a beneficial habit, put the following message on your bathroom mirror, or wherever you will see it each morning and evening:

Request Most Benevolent Outcomes Today!

You can make up one yourself on your computer or by hand, or you can go to my website, www.thegentleway-book.com, and copy and paste this saying into a document and then print it. After you have put down this book for the last time, your memory will fade. You need a physical stimulation each day to remind you to make this a habit. After it becomes a habit, you will not need to look at the reminder every day, just once a week or so to see if you have been forgetting to request them.

APPENDIX C:

RECORDING DREAMS

As I mentioned at the beginning of this appendix section, these are bonus points, things that you don't have to do to successfully request benevolent outcomes but which can really enrich your life.

I have been recording my dreams each morning since 1979—a long time! I have recorded thousands of dreams. Many times I can't recall any dreams, and the most dreams I have ever recorded in one night were nine. There are many books on dreams, so this will just be a short introduction to them.

Why record your dreams? Because most of the time they are messages from your guardian angel. I have had many precognitive dreams. One time many years ago, my wife and I were going to attend a world congress of travel agents in Manila. I had a very vivid dream of an explosion, and somehow a woman and several men were involved. Based on that dream, we cancelled our time in Manila and added extra days in Taiwan and Hong Kong. The first day of the congress, a bomb exploded at the front of the hall, injuring ten people. A woman who worked for the Philippine government in Los Angeles in some capacity and four men were arrested. That happened early on in my dream recording, so you can imagine how seriously I took it from that time onward!

During the time when my wife and I were selling our wholesale tour business, I was looking around for what I would do next. I had a vivid dream about "four-walling," which was a practice that independent filmmakers of family adventure films used in the 1970s. They would go into a town or city and rent a theater for one or several nights and advertise in newspapers, on the radio and perhaps on TV. They kept all the revenue from the box office, and the theater kept the concession stand sales. I couldn't understand why I had that dream, but before long I went into international motion picture and TV program distribution.

Most of the time, dreams are symbolic in nature. Before a Delta Airlines plane crashed at the Dallas-Fort Worth airport in August of 1985, I dreamed of a Delta-shaped aircraft crashing. Before the 1986 *Challenger* shuttle exploded during the launch, I dreamed of being in a glass capsule high above the Earth and then being under the ocean. I had three precognitive dreams before 9/11, including one where I saw a tornado going across the face of a building with a group of people floating in the air right behind it.

I use a dream dictionary to assist me in interpreting dreams. You may not need one—several of my friends and family do not—but if you do, I suggest going to your local bookstore with several dreams written down. Look those dreams up in several dream dictionaries to see which seems to be closest in interpreting your dreams, and buy that one. The book I have used for years and years is *The Dreamer's Dictionary* by Lady Stern Robinson and Tom Corbett.

To record your dreams, do the following:

1. Purchase a spiral binder, a pen with a bold point (to see in the dark) and a small pen or reading light.
2. Place them next to your bed on your nightstand.

3. Each night, record the next day's date and the town or city where you are recording the dream.

4. Say out loud, "I wish to remember my dreams tonight."

5. Buy a dream dictionary if you have a problem interpreting your dreams.

6. After a period of time of recording your dreams, you may wish to do what I do, and that is to print special binders with a hundred sheets printed front and back at a local printing place. You can go to my website, www.thegentlewaybook.com, and copy and paste the page I have already created. I like this size, as it fits on my nightstand more easily than a full spiral binder, especially with a dream dictionary, other books and magazines, your small light and a lamp already on there.

I have heard countless times over the years, "Oh, but I don't dream." That is absolutely not true. Everyone dreams. But if you don't demand that your conscious mind remembers your dreams, then they are lost immediately upon waking. Again, there are books on dreams and how to remember them, but here are a couple of suggestions:

1. Say out loud each night that you wish to remember your dreams.

2. Tell yourself to awaken five or ten minutes before your alarm goes off.

3. Try to awaken as quietly as possible. Do not turn on the radio or the TV.

4. If you awaken during the night, think about what you have been dreaming and immediately record it. You will probably not remember the dream in the morning.

5. If the dream seems to be a warning dream, say:

Most Benevolent Outcome

"I request a most benevolent outcome that if this dream [or dreams] affects my personal life, I will have a benevolent outcome. Thank you."

Good luck and good life!

MEDITATION

A nother great thing for you to try, if for no other reason than your physical health, is meditation. I have been in my doctor's office one hour after meditation, and my blood pressure count was so low that they had to retake it twice. I have done a quick version of the breathing exercise I describe below just before and during a blood pressure test/heart rate test, and have seen a drop from eighty heartbeats to sixty-six in just thirty seconds or so!

Many, many doctors recommend meditation these days. A study conducted in the fall of 2005 found that the brains of people who meditate were 5 percent thicker in the areas that deal with focus and memory than those of nonmeditators. The implication is that meditation may actually improve attention span and memory [*U.S. News and World Report*, December 26, 2005].

But meditation offers you so much more. If you have a problem in your life—and who doesn't?—you can ask your guardian angel for the solution. You just have to quiet your mind and listen for the answer.

As you progress in feeling more comfortable in your meditations, you may wish to ask all sorts of other questions about people you know and those in the news. As an example, I saw an interview on TV with Paul McCartney, and he said that he did-n't actually hear John Lennon or George Harrison say change this or that, but he implied that he felt their presence and assis-tance. So I asked in meditation what their connection with him might be, and I was told that they are now acting as guides for him and assist him in writing music. They also assist him in making other musical decisions as well.

Recently I bought the Bob Dylan documentary DVD, *No Direction Home*. I had heard his music many times over the years, but when I watched the documentary, I was impressed with the many different types of songs he composed, so I asked in a meditation about that. The message I received was that he still does not understand the "process" and thinks he just made it all up in his mind, but there were actually a number of different cosmic songwriters who contributed songs. I saw an image of a line of songwriters standing there and someone say-ing, "Next." Many of those songs helped make people think about their relations with other people.

So to begin the practice of meditation, follow these easy steps:

1. Try and choose the same time each day to meditate. This might mean you set your alarm twenty minutes earlier each morning—and yes, you may have to change your sleep time to adjust to this. Or perhaps at work after lunch, instead of watching TV or rushing off to have lunch at a restaurant, you can close the door to an office or even go into a closet.

2. Have a notebook handy where you can write down what you receive, as the messages are similar to dreams in that they will fade away quickly (I switched from a notebook to my computer due to the length of the messages).

3. I suggest that you play some nice soft music to cut down on outside noises. You may have to put headphones on

to listen. I listen to music by Robert Coxon, a Canadian
artist who plays some really beautiful music.

4. Sit comfortably in a chair, on a sofa or on the floor. Sit in
   an upright position—don't slump. Ask for a benevolent
   outcome for your meditation.

5. Close your eyes. Put the tips of both thumbs and forefin-
   gers together.

6. Begin breathing in through your nose, holding to a count
   of four, and then gently blowing out through your mouth,
   with your lips just barely open. This helps center your
   attention. After a little time, continue to breathe in through
   your nose and out your mouth without holding the breath.

7. At the same time, relax your body, allowing your muscles
   to relax from the bottom of your feet slowly up through
   your legs, your torso, your arms, your hands and your
   neck. Most importantly, relax those mouth muscles.

8. Start purposefully to quiet your mind. Push any thoughts
   of your many daily activities gently away. This is the
   hardest part. It will take you some practice, because
   your mind will want to jump around to a hundred different subjects.

9. As you quiet your mind, imagine a beautiful white light
   filled with pure love coming from your guardian angel
   down through the top of your head. This will help you
   focus. Let this beautiful loving light from your angel travel
   slowly through your whole body—first down through your
   head, then to your throat, then through your heart and
   solar plexus, then through your stomach, past your groin
   area and on down through your feet. Imagine it going
   through the floor all the way to the center of the Earth.

10. Now imagine a golden light going out from your heart
    and surrounding your whole body in a spiral motion, like

a cocoon. Then expand the light and imagine it going all the way around the world. All of this is helping you focus and visualize.

11. Now, while still gently breathing in through your nose and out through your mouth, imagine yourself walking down a set of stairs. The stairs have numbers on them. Go from seven all the way down to one. As you walk down the stairs, think, "Seven, down, down, down, six, down, down, down," and so on. If you feel the need, go down another set of seven stairs.

12. At this point, you can keep your mind quiet and imagine yourself in some beautiful quiet place like a beach or a mountain. See if there are messages or images that come to your mind. Or if you have a question, gently ask it in your mind and then *wait for the answer.* Don't jump to another subject or let any other thoughts distract you. It will seem as if you are thinking the answer, but you're not.

13. When you feel it is time to come back, imagine to yourself that you are walking back up the stairs, and as you count from one to seven, you will be fully awake. Record any feelings, images and messages that you received.

Don't become frustrated if your first few attempts do not seem to have results. This is like riding a bike. It takes a little practice, but do you remember how much fun it was to ride that bike successfully? This is even better!

There are books on meditation if you wish to take it further and learn more about it. If you want to buy a meditation CD, you can go to www.dicksutphen.com. In my opinion, Dick has one of the best voices I have ever heard. Choose one of his several guided meditation CDs for a most benevolent outcome for your meditations!

WARM-HEART MEDITATION

T his is a meditation whose purpose is to acquaint you with the feeling of physically and mentally loving yourself. After I give you the directions for this seemingly simple exercise, I will describe the many benefits that can result from doing this.

Close your eyes. Take your thumb and rub it very gently across your fingertips for about one minute while doing nothing else. Notice that it focuses your attention on your physical body and away from all the other things around you.

Next, bring that same physical attention toward your heart or anywhere in that area where you can look for or generate a warm feeling. This might not be your heart; it could be your solar plexus or abdomen. It may take a minute or two to find or generate warmth that you can feel.

Go into that warmth, and stay with it and feel it for a few minutes so that you can memorize this method and so your body can create a memory of how it feels and how it needs to feel for you. At different times, it might be in different places. Don't try and move it; just feel it. As you continue to repeat this exercise, you will be able to do it for longer periods of time.

Afterward, think about this: *The warmth is the physical evidence of loving yourself.* You have read for years about how we need to love ourselves, but most of these have been mental concepts. This is a physical experience of loving yourself. It unites you with your angels and all of creation. It will provide you with a greater ease and comfort in life.

You may notice as you get better at this that your friends and acquaintances will be more relaxed around you and that things seem to be more harmonious. You will tend to not become upset as much as you used to. Animals may react differently to you—they will be more friendly and relaxed around you, perhaps looking at you differently. This is because you are radiating out this warm love energy.

Do not try and send this to other people. If they are interested in what you are doing or why they feel better around you, you can teach them this simple meditation. Again, this will benefit you and improve your experience along the Gentle Way.

APPENDIX F:

COMMUNICATING WITH PETS AND ANIMALS

I received the following information from two American Indian shamans. Many of you have seen TV programs about pet psychics and wished that you could communicate with your loving dog, cat or other animal. How many times has your pet looked up at you and you just know that it is trying to tell you something?

According to these two shamans, animals communicate not in words but in pictures. If you have been requesting benevolent outcomes for a while, then your awareness and ability to receive these pictures will be better than if you just begin immediately.

If you've been at work all day, when you arrive home and greet your pet, relax your mind and see if you can see any pictures of what your pet has been doing while you were away. Then create a simple picture in your mind of what you've been doing, and send your pet pictures of how much you love it. Make simple pictures, not complicated ones.

When you take your pet to the veterinarian, send it pictures that it will be taken care of. Your pet picks up so much fear in animals there, and this frightens it too. Send your pet calming pictures.

If you do receive words, they are being communicated through your guardian angel or guides. Then your pet or animal may be trying to teach you something. Animals are much more intelligent than we have given them credit for.

If you meet a wild animal while you are out hiking—and there are wild animals in the city, such as squirrels and rodents—stop and maintain a respectful distance. The animal will wait a moment for you to introduce yourself. If you do not, then the animal may give you an introduction, showing you what it did that day over ten to twenty seconds. You can then respond with simple pictures of what you did.

Then there is a quiet time when the animal sits or hunkers down, and you can do the same. The animal might send you pictures of its family, and you can do the same. It might have a message for you about the trail—possibly it is dangerous to go the way you're headed. Just be open.

Perhaps someone reading these words will be the next "horse whisperer" or "pet psychic"—a most benevolent outcome for your efforts!

APPENDIX G:

A LIVING PRAYER FOR DISASTERS

I have placed this living prayer last in the book so that you can easily reference it whenever you feel a compassionate need to assist those people in another part of the world. This can be said for earthquakes, tsunamis, volcanic eruptions, hurricanes, tornadoes, terrorist attacks or any other calamity for which you wish to request angelic assistance.

If you recall, I wrote earlier that you do not want to limit this living prayer just to human beings. By saying "all those beings," you not only include humans but rescue dogs, cats, animals and angelic beings. And for those of you who doubt how animals can assist humans, I just recently saw a TV news story about a cat who saved its incapacitated human companion by dialing 911!

Living Prayer

"I am asking that all those beings who need help in _____ recieve all the help they need right now from all those beings who can help them. Thank you!"

GLOSSARY:

Definitions of Terms as They Are Used in This Book

ANGELS: Divine intermediaries who assist in arranging benevolent outcomes and living prayers.

ANGEL SPEAK: Words such as "benevolent" and "living prayer" that seem to be used in the angelic world.

BENEVOLENT (BE-NEV-O-LENT): A kindly disposition to promote happiness and prosperity through good works, or by generosity in and pleasure of doing good works [definition from *Webster's Dictionary*].

GUARDIAN ANGEL: An angel who volunteers to watch over a particular person throughout his or her life.

GUIDES: Angelic entities who assist a guardian angel in giving guidance to an individual. These can include deceased parents, relatives or friends.

HIGHER SELF: Your soul.

HOPE: Desire accompanied by the expectation of obtaining what is desired or belief that it is obtainable. [definition from *Webster's Dictionary*].

LIVING PRAYER: A request made to your guardian angel and other angelic beings when it is for others. This may include you as well.

MBO: Abbreviation for "most benevolent outcome."

ABOUT THE AUTHOR

Tom T. Moore is in the entertainment business, where for the past twenty-four years he has been president and CEO of his own international motion picture and TV program distribution business, based in Dallas, Texas. During this time, he has co-executive-produced several movies and TV shows, and has traveled extensively as part of his business duties to international film markets held in Cannes, France; Milan, Italy; Los Angeles, California; and Budapest, Hungary. He brings a keen knowledge of how requesting benevolent outcomes can be used both in business affairs and in one's personal life, and relates many personal stories regarding these requests. He says that requesting benevolent outcomes for over the past ten years has resulted in his leading a more gentle, less stressful and less fearful life—the Gentle Way!

Before becoming an international film distributor, Moore owned and operated an international wholesale tour company with his wife, selling tours through three thousand travel agents nationwide. That business began out of his first successful venture, a ski club for single adults, which grew to be the largest snow ski club in Texas. Moore is still an avid skier and loves to ski in the United States, Canada and Europe.

Moore graduated with a Bachelors of Business Administration in finance from Texas Christian University in Fort Worth, Texas, and served in the U.S. Army as a first lieutenant. He is a native of Dallas, Texas, and is married with two children.

To book Tom T. Moore as a speaker at your next conference or event, email him at **speaker@TheGentleWayBook.com**.

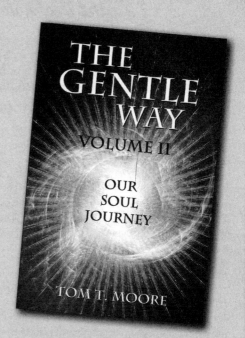

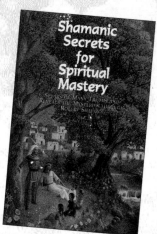